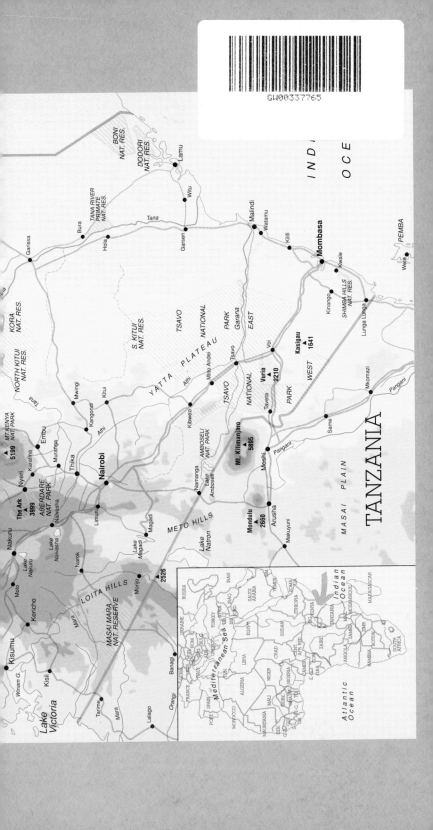

GW00337765

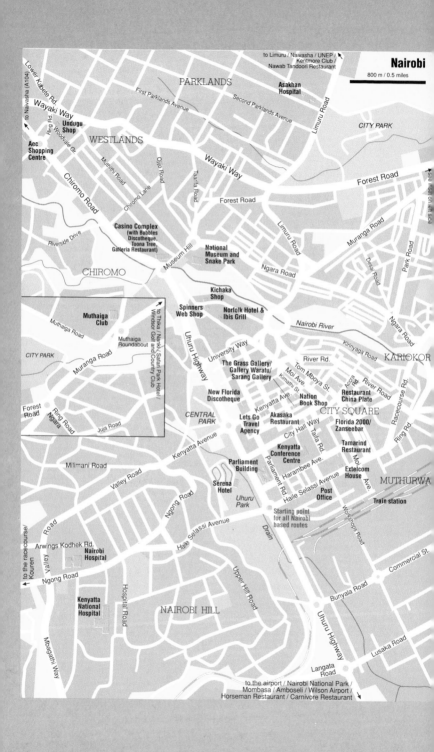

Nairobi

800 m / 0.5 miles

PARKLANDS

WESTLANDS

CHIROMO

to Limuru / Naivasha / UNEP /
Kentmore Club
Nawab Tandoori Restaurant

Asakhan
Hospital

CITY PARK

First Parklands Avenue

Second Parklands Avenue

Lower Kabete Rd

Wayaki Way

Ring Rd.

Woodvale Gr.

Undugu
Shop

Aec
Shopping
Centre

Chiromo Road

Muthithi Road

Ojijo Road

Chiromo Lane

Taarifa Road

Wayaki Way

Forest Road

Forest Road

Limuru Road

Muranga Road

Park Road

Dessai Road

Ngara Road

Riverside Drive

Casino Complex
(with Bubbles
Discotheque,
Toona Tree,
Galleria Restaurant)

Museum Hill

National
Museum and
Snake Park

Kichaka
Shop

Spinners
Web Shop

Norfolk Hotel &
Ibis Grill

Nairobi River

Ngara Road

Muthaiga
Club

Muthaiga Road

Muthaiga
Roundabout

to Thika / Nanki / Satan Park Hotel /
Windsor Golf and Country Club

CITY PARK

Muranga Road

Forest
Road

Ring Road

Ngara

Juja Road

Milimani Road

Valley Road

Ngong Road

Uhuru Highway

University Way

The Grass Gallery/
Gallery Waratu/
Sarang Gallery

New Florida
Discotheque

CENTRAL
PARK

Lets Go
Travel
Agency

Kenyatta Avenue

River Rd.

Tom Mboya St.

Moi Ave.

Kimathi St.

Kenyatta Ave.

Nation
Book Shop

Akasaka
Restaurant

City Hall Way

Taita Rd.

Restaurant
China Plate

CITY SQUARE

Florida 2000/
Zanseebar

Tamarind
Restaurant

Kirinyaga Road

KARIOKOR

Accra Rd.

River Road

Racecourse Rd.

Ring Rd.

Moi Ave.

Kenyatta
Conference
Centre

Harambee Ave.

Parliament Rd.

Parliament
Building

Serena
Hotel

Uhuru
Park

Haile Selassi Avenue

Post
Office

Extelcom
House

MUTHURWA

Train station

Starting point
for all Nairobi
based routes

Drain

Haile Selassi Avenue

Workshop Road

Road

Valley

Arwings Kodhek Rd.

Nairobi
Hospital

Ngong Road

Hospital Road

Upper Hill Road

Bunyala Road

Commercial St.

Kenyatta
National
Hospital

NAIROBI HILL

Uhuru Highway

Mbagathi Way

Langata
Road

Lusaka Road

to the racecourse/
Kouren

to the airport / Nairobi National Park /
Mombasa / Amboseli / Wilson Airport /
Horseman Restaurant / Carnivore Restaurant

to Naivasha (A104)

Lower Kabete Rd (A104)

Forest Road

see map on left side

INSIGHT *pocket* GUIDES

Kenya

Written and Presented by **Marti Colley**

INSIGHT
pocket
GUIDES

Insight Pocket Guide:

KENYA

Directed by
Hans Höfer

Managing Editor
Andrew Eames

Photography by
David Keith Jones and others

Design Concept by
V.Barl

Design by
Carlotta Junger

© 1994 APA Publications (HK) Ltd

All Rights Reserved

Printed in Singapore by
Höfer Press (Pte) Ltd
Fax: 65-8616438

Distributed in the UK & Ireland by
GeoCenter International UK Ltd
The Viables Center, Harrow Way
Basingstoke, Hampshire RG22 4BJ
ISBN: 9-62421-584-7

Worldwide distribution enquiries:
Höfer Communications Pte Ltd
38 Joo Koon Road
Singapore 2262
ISBN: 9-62421-584-7

NO part of this book may be reproduced,
stored in a retrieval system or transmitted in any form
or means electronic, mechanical, photocopying,
recording or otherwise, without prior written
permission of Apa Publications. Brief text quotations
with use of photographs are exempted for book review
purposes only.
As every effort is made to provide accurate information
in this publication, we would appreciate it if readers
would call our attention to any errors that may occur by
communicating with Apa Villa, 81 The Cut, London
SE1 8LL. Tel: 71-620-0008, Fax: 71-620-1074.
Information has been obtained from sources believed
to be reliable, but its accuracy and completeness,
and the opinions based thereon, are not guaranteed.

KARIBU!

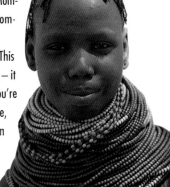

Marti Colley

I still don't know how I came to live in Kenya. One day, fresh from college, I was driving through Africa, smitten with the travel bug and heading who knows where. The next, I was unloading my backpack, waving my friends goodbye, unable to leave. Now I live and work as a consultant writer/editor for the United Nations Environment Programme in Nairobi.

Even with my itchy feet I felt that Kenya was not a country to be rushed through, but rather a land to savour. I am not alone in feeling this way. Every year around one million tourists come to visit Kenya. They come for the game animals, or to swim in the Indian Ocean, or to climb the second-highest mountain in Africa or to journey through the desert. They travel by car or on horses, camels, mountain bike or foot. They stay in lodges, luxury hotels and traditional safari camps. Whoever they are, whatever they do, there's a niche to suit them in Kenya.

In this book I've suggested how to see elephant, lion, buffalo, leopard, rhino and others; how to go up in a balloon, horseback ride among the game, climb Mount Kenya and deep-sea fish in tropical seas. I've also given details of a back route to Northern Kenya, up to remote Lake Turkana — the birthplace of mankind.

All these itineraries are based on either Nairobi or Mombasa, and include precise road directions and recommendations key to your enjoyment.

Kenya is an isle of tranquillity in a sea of unrest. This stems, in part, from the common outlook: _pole pole_ — it means slowly slowly — is the only way to go. So if you're looking to unwind and forget the pressures of home, you've come to the right place. There's no hurry in Africa. _Karibu — Welcome!_

Contents

*Preceding pages: wildebeest
on the move, Masai Mara*

*Following pages: sun-soaking in
a coastal resort*

HISTORY &

Kenya's Rift Valley is rightly named the 'Cradle of Mankind'. Clues to man's earliest history were unearthed there in the 1960s when anthropologists Mary and Louis Leakey found the remains of a large-brained hominid with gripping thumbs that put back the believed origins of man by about 1½ million years. The remains are still the object of some controversy although later finds by the Leakeys' son, Richard, who is head of the Kenya Wildlife Services, seem to confirm that primitive man was around much earlier than was originally thought.

The history of the next few thousand centuries is not very clear.

Kenya was on one of the major immigration routes through Africa and, beginning around 2,000BC, successive waves of Cushitic, Bantu and Nilotic peoples passed through, bringing with them tool-making and agricultural skills.

These are the ancestors of the more than 40 different peoples who make up the modern Kenya, and have made the country a virtual paradise for archaeologists and anthropologists.

Early man

Culture

Arab Influence

In the 9th century, even as migrations continued in the interior, down at the coast Mombasa and Malindi were already important commercial and trade centres between India, Arabia and Africa. Their development received a boost with the emergence of the Prophet Mohammed which sent political and religious dissidents flocking south, bringing with them the Arab architecture and Islamic culture that still dominate Kenya's coastal towns today. Trade flourished and the next five or six centuries were boom years as Mombasa, Malindi and Lamu became centres of all that was new – technology, business, literature, arts and crafts. It is around this time that Kiswahili – a mixture of Arabic and the vernacular – is believed to have developed.

Arab domination continued until 1498 when Vasco da Gama arrived, looking for a sea route from Portugal to India. At first, the Arabs repelled his fleet from Mombasa but he was welcomed by the sultan at Malindi, who loaded his ships with riches and gave him a guide to Calcutta. Elsewhere on the coast the Arabs had to pay bitterly for their lack of hospitality. In the early 16th century and for the following 200 years Mom-

Arab influence on a dhow

basa was repeatedly attacked and reduced to rubble and rebuilt. In 1593 the Portuguese began construction of Fort Jesus in Mombasa and over the next century they consolidated their position along the coast. It wasn't until 1696 that the Arabs started to fight back successfully and it took them until 1729 to drive the Portuguese out. Then the Arabs once again dominated trade in the area until the British and Germans arrived at the end of the 19th century.

For the next 100 years the coast was ruled by the imam of Oman except for a brief, three-year interlude from 1824 when an overzealous British captain made Mombasa a Protectorate of the Crown of England. This was later repudiated and power passed back to Oman until the late 1880s.

By this time Oman's court had moved to Zanzibar and the British and Germans, aware of the wealth of the East African coast, had begun trading in the region. In 1886, both Britain and Germany agreed that the Omani sultan would rule the Kenyan coast up to a depth of 10 miles, but it would remain as a British Protectorate. It stayed this way until 1963 when the ruling sultan handed it over to the newly independent Kenya.

Colonials and the Interior

Until the 1880s the Kenyan interior remained closed to outsiders who were afraid of the dominant Maasai tribe and their reputation for ferocity. However, European explorers had already penetrated other African interiors and Kenya could not remain inviolate for long. By 1883 Joseph Thompson had 'discovered' the Rift Valley lakes and travelled as far as Lake Victoria. Two years later, Bishop James Hannington 'found' Lake Bogoria. By this time Maasai strength had been depleted by disease and clan fighting so the British were able to negotiate a treaty allowing them to build a railway right through the centre of Maasai grazing lands, from Mombasa to Nairobi and on to Lake Victoria. It was finally completed in 1901.

The railway was symbolic of the race to colonise Africa. Its aim was to set up communications with Uganda before the Germans and so establish British dominance in the region. The British Parliament described the scheme as a waste of both time and money and 'a lunatic line to nowhere'. But the project went ahead anyway at a massive cost to the British taxpayer of £9,500 a mile.

Maasai chief negotiates with the British, 1898

To make a return on what was, in those days, a very substantial investment, Europeans were encouraged to settle and farm the land along the railway line. This was the start of the era when renegade minor British aristocrats and other 'White Highlanders' came to start afresh in the Aberdare mountains, which offered the best prospects for arable development. By 1912 the Protectorate was paying its own way.

Following World War I, the British government began the Soldier Settlement Scheme – in which estates in the White Highlands were given away in a lottery or sold for peanuts to white veterans of the European campaign. The Africans who had fought alongside the Europeans were offered nothing. By the 1950s over 80,000 Europeans had settled in Kenya.

The Struggle for Freedom

Not surprisingly the native Kenyans were unhappy with government practices which took land away from Africans to give to white settlers. In the 1920s, as more repressive laws were enforced, they formed their first political parties with the ultimate aim of taking over from the British and running the country for themselves. This was the start of the struggle for *Uhuru* – freedom.

It was a struggle that took many years to win. After World War II, demobbed African soldiers returned to Kenya in militant frame of mind, fully trained in the use of arms and having realised that the Europeans were not all-powerful. They campaigned actively for changes under the leadership of Jomo Kenyatta who had lived in self-imposed exile in London for the last 15 years, where he had pleaded the African cause with the Colonial Secretary.

Jomo Kenyatta

For the next seven years the calls for change became more vociferous until, frustrated by the lack of action, a guerilla movement – *Mau Mau* – was formed. Its members swore to kill those who supported the colonial regime. The first deaths – of 21 Kikuyus (Bantu-speaking farmers) loyal to the British – came in 1953 and the bloodshed continued up to 1956, by which time some 13,500 Africans and 100 Europeans had died and more than 20,000 Kikuyus were detained in special camps. The colonial government accused Kenyatta, probably unjustly, of leading the *Mau Mau* campaign and he was jailed until 1959. But although *Mau Mau* was effectively suppressed, it was clear that colonialism had had its day.

In 1960 the Lancaster House Conference was held in London at which it was agreed that power should be transferred to a democratically-elected black government. Having successfully united to get rid of white oppression, the Kenyans now began to argue among themselves over the divisions of power. When independence came on 12 December 1963, Jomo Kenyatta, leader of the Kikuyus, was elected president.

Stability and Democracy

Kenyatta ruled for the next 15 years and steered Kenya towards stability and prosperity, certainly in African terms. At first, his policies induced rapid economic growth and there was a mood of optimism for Kenya's future prosperity. By 1970 two-thirds of European-owned land had been sold to the government in obligatory land sales and was then handed over to 50,000 landless peasants as subsistence plots.

Internationally, Kenya was seen as a model of African stability and democracy. However, back home an elite group of profiteers had emerged who exploited their connections with the president to milk the country dry, notably through ivory trading. Kenyatta's wife, Mama Ngina, is widely thought to have been involved. Besides nepotism, Kenyatta's worse failing was his inability to accept honest criticism. Many of those who spoke out against him were detained without trial. Other critics met mysterious deaths.

On Kenyatta's death in 1978 he was succeeded by Vice President Daniel arap Toroitich Moi. During the first 10 years of his reign, Moi consolidated his hold on power through increased oppression and intolerance of political opposition. He amended the constitution to make Kenya officially a one-party state – which led to an unsuccessful coup attempt by the Air Force in 1982 – and in 1987 gave himself the power to appoint and dismiss members of the judiciary. By the end of the decade Moi had no effective political opposition, other than a few outspoken members of the clergy who used their Sunday sermons to attack injustices of the regime. Corruption was rife and the standard of living was falling. There was growing discontent but most Kenyans were too afraid to talk.

Events came to a head in 1990 when the collapse of communism in Eastern Europe opened Kenyan eyes to the possibility of political change. At first Moi used paramilitary security units to crack down on pro-democracy demonstrations and had opposition leaders arrested and detained without trial. However, the pop-

Daniel arap Moi

Wildlife made tame; Turkana milking their camel

ular movement for political change continued to gain momentum and received a boost when Western powers, faced with the global recession, were forced to choose between regenerating Eastern European economies or continuing to support undemocratic African regimes. One by one diplomatic missions announced that aid to Kenya was to be frozen until multi-party elections were held.

These elections took place in December 1992 and President Moi was re-elected for a third four-year term, though he polled less than 50 percent of the vote. Three months later the Kenyan shilling collapsed, largely as a result of all the millions of extra money that was printed prior to the elections and spent, so it is alleged, on persuading Kenyans to vote for Moi. Economic hardship for many Kenyans is bound to follow and it remains to be seen if Moi can maintain his control over Kenyan politics in a multi-party era.

Wildlife Preservation – and Poaching

In the past, man lived in close harmony with the environment. The earliest hunter-gatherers had a healthy respect for wildlife and killed only to eat or as a religious ritual – to kill an animal without reason was to violate all that was sacred and to call for retribution from the powers above.

Five thousand years ago nomadic herder immigrants from Ethiopia and the Nile Valley brought domestic livestock into Kenya. They began to live in symbiosis with the indigenous hunter-gatherers, trading milk, use of land and protection for wildlife products and labour. These early herders accepted the right of animals other than cattle, sheep and goats to share land and water resources. Today, three-quarters of Kenya is still inhabited by herders and pastoralists.

The concept of land ownership and large-scale commercial

17

farming was introduced with the movement of Europeans into the hinterland of Kenya in the late 19th century. So began Kenya's massive transformation into an environment manipulated by man.

Some modification was beneficial and non-destructive – such as the early burning of grasslands, which cleared the regenerating shrubs and ensured that new grass could benefit from the rain. Other modifications left lasting marks – for example, forest-clearing on steep slopes and the over-exploiting of vulnerable species like elephant, rhino, lion, leopard and cheetah for the pleasure of hunting and financial gain.

The development of modern medicine led to a population explosion in the early 20th century which put tremendous pressures on natural resources, particularly wildlife. Increasing numbers of species and their habitats became threatened with extinction.

Following the mass destruction of World War II, there was worldwide concern about conserving the earth's biodiversity. Kenya was one of the first countries to take action – by conserving the environment and wildlife of the Athi River plains on the outskirts of Nairobi in the nation's first national park, gazetted in 1945. Twenty years later Kenya had one of the best systems of national parks in the world, which was one reason why the United Nations made Nairobi the base for their Environment Programme (UNEP) in the early 1970s. Today, nearly 8 percent of Kenya's land area is protected and this excludes the miles of coastal marine parks.

Mass poaching of elephant and rhino in the years up to 1990 was fuelled by demands for ivory and rhino horn from markets in the South East. By 1990, fewer than 500 of Kenya's 70,000 rhinos and only around 15 percent of her elephant population were still alive. Then the Kenya Wildlife Service was set up under the leadership of Dr Richard Leakey who brought over crack British SAS troops to train armed game-rangers and instigated a shoot-to-kill policy on anyone trespassing in game parks. After the deaths of several poachers, the numbers of rhino and elephant are slowly increasing.

To demonstrate Kenya's on-going commitment to protect wildlife, hundreds of tons of illegally poached ivory which had been recovered by the Kenya Wildlife Service was set alight in 1990 in Nairobi National Park.

Tusk fire in 1990

Historical Highlights

1.8 million BC Ancestral hominids living on the shores of Lake Turkana – the 'cradle of mankind'.

500,000 Cushitic, Nilotic and Bantu peoples, the ancestors of present day Kenyans, move in from all over the continent.

AD110 Diogenes the Greek records details of trade in Mombasa during the rule of King Muza. This is the first known description of the Kenyan coast.

900 Arrival of Islam, marking the beginning of the coast's golden age.

14th century Swahili community emerges. Arab and Persian settlers develop coastal trade and caravan routes to the interior.

1498 Vasco da Gama arrives in Malindi, signalling the start of Portuguese influence which ends in 1696 with the beginning of the siege of Fort Jesus by the Arabs.

1824 The British ship, *HMS Leven*, brings Captain Owen to Mombasa and claims Kenya as a British Protectorate. This marks the start of the British influence. Three years later the Protectorate is repudiated and influence is surrendered to Oman.

mid-1800s British anti-slavery campaign is at its height.

1849 First European sighting of Mount Kenya – by Austrian Johan Ludwig Krapf.

1880 Joseph Thompson sets out to walk 'Through Maasai Land' (title of his book) at the bequest of the British Royal Geographical Society. He charts much of modern Kenya.

1886 Kenya and Uganda are assigned to the British at the Berlin Conference.

1892 Johnstone Kamau, later to change his name to Jomo Kenyatta, is born in the Highlands north of Nairobi.

1896 Construction of the 'Lunatic Line' rail link from Mombasa to Uganda begins. It takes six years to complete and ends at Lake Victoria.

1918 End of World War I. British government offers war veterans land in the Kenyan Highlands as part of a settlement scheme.

1922 Harry Thuku, leader of the first pan-Kenyan nationalist organisation, is arrested. Between 21 and 100 protesting Kenyans are massacred outside central police station, Nairobi.

1929 Jomo Kenyatta goes to England to plead East African Association's cause.

1939 World War II – Kenya used as a base and training ground for operations in Ethiopia (then Abyssinia) by the British.

1944 Start of *Mau Mau* – an underground independence movement with an oath of allegiance against the British.

1952 Simmering Kenyan nationalism. A state of emergency is called following attacks against white settlers. Jomo Kenyatta and other leaders are arrested and imprisoned.

1959 Kenyatta released and put under house arrest.

1963 Kenya gains independence (*Uhuru*). Jomo Kenyatta is elected as first president.

1964 Kenya declared a republic.

1978 Daniel Toroitich arap Moi becomes president on death of Kenyatta.

1982 Attempted coup led by rebels in the Kenyan Air Force. Constitional amendments make Kenya a one-party state.

1992 Following changes in Eastern Europe, Kenyans call for political plurality. The first multi-party elections since independence are held. President Moi is re-elected, against allegations of ballot-rigging.

1993 Kenyan shilling devalued by around 50 percent.

Day itine

Most visitors to Kenya divide their time between the game parks of the interior and the superb beaches along the coast. Reflecting this pattern, the itineraries in this guidebook are grouped around two bases: Nairobi, which is well placed for the wildlife, and Mombasa, the hub of the coast. For advice on travelling between these two bases, see *Practical Information*.

The Nairobi section includes the bulk of the 'safaris', with itineraries ranging from half a day to seven days. They assume the use of private transport (unless otherwise specified), and where a four-wheel-drive vehicle is required it is mentioned in the itinerary's opening text. Inevitably, in view of the limited road network, some of the longer itineraries pass sights and attractions which are also covered in day or half-day options, so it is sensible to read and compare itineraries before setting off. If you want to take in as much as possible in just seven days, I recommend the 'Grand Tour' (Itinerary 16), though this does not include the Masai Mara.

If you are interested in seeing specific wildlife, it is worth studying the Wildlife Checklist (see pages 68–71), which will tell you where to go.

Note: You should book accommodation in advance; details of addresses and telephone numbers are given in each itinerary.

Heading north

FROM NAIROBI

Nairobi is pleasant enough but it doesn't offer much to the visitor. Most of the itineraries that follow are therefore devoted to destinations easily reached from Nairobi. If you want to see more of the city itself, try the following:

◆ A mini coach tour of Nairobi and environs (Tel: 02-227847/8 or 331960).

Nairobi curio shop

◆ Visit the Parliament building (Parliament Road, near City Square; Tel: 02-221291 ext. 254/5) and, when Parliament is in session, take a seat in the public or Speaker's Gallery to watch democracy, Kenyan-style, in action.

◆ Walk around the Arboretum to see a wonderful collection of tropical trees and shrubs (Arboretum Road, off State House Road; Tel: 02-722620; open daylight hours; admission free).

◆ On Sundays go to the races at Ngong Racecourse and see all the old colonials parading in their finery (Tel: 02-566108/9).

◆ Travel on horseback out from Karen to the edge of the Rift Valley – full-day and half-day treks (Tel: 02-225255).

◆ For good aerial photographs of Nairobi, take pictures from the top floor of the Kenyatta International Conference Centre.

1. In and Around Nairobi

A morning in the National Museum and Snake Park, followed by lunch in an Italian restaurant. Afternoon trip to the Animal Orphanage and Nairobi National Park.

From Kenyatta Avenue drive along Uhuru Highway. At the second roundabout turn right up Museum Hill. Just before the crest of the hill turn right into the museum car park.

The **National Museum** is a fascinating introduction to Kenya's eclectic culture and history. In particular, don't miss the early man section, Joy Adamson's flower paintings or the collection of tribal artifacts (weapons, ceremonial objects, etc) in the upstairs gallery. There's also a hall of stuffed animals (most of them shot in the colonial era) and a contemporary Kenyan art gallery. Aim to spend a couple of hours in all browsing here.

The **Snake Park** is opposite the museum, on the other side of the

The National Museum

car park. See green and black mambas, spitting cobras, pythons and other snakes from Africa and the Americas, as well as crocodile, giant tortoise, turtles and lizards. You should spend 45 minutes here.

Afterwards, come out of the museum car park, turn left on to Museum Hill, drive down and all the way around the roundabout and back up Museum Hill. Turn first left into the Casino complex and drive to the end of the car park. Have lunch followed by a cappuccino coffee and Italian cake and ice-cream in the **Toona Tree** restaurant (see *Eating Out*).

The game part of this day should start after lunch and last till sundown (around 6.30pm). Late afternoon and early mornings are the best times to sight game and also the best times for taking photographs, when the sun is no longer directly overhead and shadows are becoming longer. Buy the Macmillan Kenya Traveller's Map – it includes a good map of Nairobi National Park. Maps are also available from the snack kiosk sited at the park entrance.

To get to the park from Kenyatta Avenue, turn left on to Uhuru Highway. At the third roundabout turn right on to Langata Road. Drive for 6½ kms (4 miles). The

Orphan chimp

entrance to Nairobi National Park is on the left, about 15 minutes from the city centre. If you've opted to go to see your game in the morning, visit this first and the Animal Orphanage afterwards. If it's an afternoon excursion visit the Orphanage first so that you're in the National Park at sundown.

The **Animal Orphanage** is before the toll gate at the main entrance of Nairobi National Park, on the right (open daily 8am–6pm). It's home to young, sick and injured animals which are cared for until they are strong enough to fend for themselves in the wild. There are also a few resident exotics such as tigers, a chimpanzee and a gorilla which were given to Kenya by foreign governments, and a Wildlife Education Centre and Museum.

Nairobi National Park (open daily 6am–7pm, last admission 6.15pm; Tel: 02-501081) covers 117 sq km (44 sq miles) and is fenced only on the northern and western boundaries. Consequently the game, which includes buffalo, black rhino, leopard, lion and hippos in a pool in the southeast, as well as all the usual plains game (gazelles, impala, zebra, giraffe, etc) is free to come and go as it pleases. At the park entrance ask the keepers if there have been any special sightings of particular animals that day so that you know which circuits to follow.

2. Limuru and Mrs Mitchell

Half-day excursion to the tea plantations of Limuru, visiting the grave of Louis Leakey. Mrs Mitchell's talk on tea and early days in Kenya. Afterwards to the Waterfall, and then the Kentmere Club for tea.

–The journey from Nairobi takes about half an hour–

From Kenyatta Avenue turn right on to Uhuru Highway. At the second roundabout turn right up Museum Hill, past the casino. Drive straight on to the T-junction then turn left and drive through the valley into **Muthaiga**. Drive past Muthaiga *dukas* (shops) and garage on the left and turn left at the round-about on to Limuru Road (c62). Keep going straight through Gigiri, past the signboards for the United Nations, Runda Estate, Gringos Tex-Mex restaurant (great for frozen margaritas and with a 'Happy Hour' from 4–7pm) and on to **Ruaka** village. Turn right here,

Limuru tea-pickers

A bronze sunbird in Limuru

following the signboards for the Kentmere Club and Waterfalls and Picnic Site. Drive through the villages of Muchatha and Banana Hill and past the Kentmere Club. Turn right into Limuru Girls' School Road.

Stop at the **All Saints' Church**, on the left a few metres after the turn-off, where the celebrated archaeologist/anthropologist, Louis Leakey, is buried. With his wife, Mary, Leakey discovered the oldest-known skull of ancient man in a gorge in Tanzania, putting back the believed orgins of man by about 1½ million years. The discovery and its conclusions are still controversial. It is said locally that once a year the sun shines directly through the church's rose window and casts a halo on the altar.

Come out of All Saints' churchyard and turn left to continue up Limuru Girls' School Road to Kiambethu Farm, on the left, not far after Limuru Girls' School – look out for the signboard with 'Mitchell' on it.

Kiambethu Farm was built by white settler Albert Butler McDonnel who arrived in Kenya at the turn of the century and set up one of the first tea plantations on land he had bought for a penny an acre. His eldest daughter, Evelyn Mitchell, now 80-something, still lives there and gives a fascinating talk about tea and colonial life in the old days, followed by a short stroll in her few acres of indigenous forest.

Local coffee

She'll show you black and white colobus monkeys, countless birds and tell you the names and traditional uses of many of the trees. Back at the house, ask to see Mrs Mitchell's photo album with sepia prints of the railway station, picnics, parties and other social events in the Nairobi of the 1920s and before. Mrs Mitchell is understandably frail, but with luck she will continue to receive visitors to her home for some time to come.

After lunch in the garden

drive back a few hundred metres along Limuru Girls' School Road and turn left at the signs to visit the **Waterfall**. This is a short but quite steep stroll from the picnic site and is best avoided on Sundays when too many Nairobi residents drive up from the city to spend the afternoon here.

I suggest you then go on to the **Kentmere Club** for tea and to check out their amazing menu (you'll want to come back here for dinner) and gardens.

To return to Nairobi, turn left out of the Kentmere and then a few hundred metres later take the first turn on the right. This road winds down through the valley, past slopes planted with coffee, and a saw-mill. At the T-junction turn left on to the (c62) Limuru Road and drive back, through the villages of Ruaka and Muthaiga into town.

3. Out of Africa

A full-day excursion to the Ostrich Park and Arts and Craft Village, Giraffe Manor, Karen Blixen Museum, Horseman Restaurant and the Bomas of Kenya.

If you enjoyed the book or film *Out of Africa* and want to see for yourself Karen Blixen's house at the foot of the Ngong Hills, this is the circuit for you.

From Kenyatta Avenue turn left on to Uhuru Highway. At the third roundabout turn right on to Langata Road. Drive past the Army barracks and Nairobi National Park to the crossroads with Langata Road South on the left. Turn right – it is clearly signposted – for the **Ostrich Park and Arts and Craft Village** (Tel: Nairobi 02-891051, open 9am–5.30pm all week).

This is probably the closest you'll ever get to ostriches. Feed them bunches of grass provided by the informative gamekeepers. After cooing over the ostrich chicks, look around the **Arts and Crafts Village**, whose collection of unusual and striking things includes butterflies, flowers and fishing flies made from flamingo feathers, woven rugs and baskets, jewellery and carvings. The resident crafts-people are happy to let you try your hand at their art.

Giraffe Manor

From the Ostrich Park, go back to Langata Road and turn right, then immediately first left. Follow the signs to the Giraffe Manor/African Fund for Endangered Wildlife (AFEW), off Koitobus

Road. The **Giraffe Manor** (Tel: 02-891658; open daily 9.00am–5.30pm) was set up to save the endangered Rothschild or Ugandan giraffe whose natural habitat in Northern Uganda/Southern Sudan was being threatened by agricultural cultivation. Feed the resident beasts with peanuts provided by the warden from a raised platform which puts you on a level with their enormous heads and even more enormous tongues. Have morning coffee here.

Afterwards drive back to Langata Road and turn left. Continue as far as Karen Road on your left. Turn here and drive for about 2½km (1½ miles) until you reach the **Karen Blixen Museum** (Tel: 882779; open daily, 9.30am–6.30pm). Although this is the actual house where she lived and which is described in *Out of Africa*, not much remains of Karen Blixen's original possessions (most of them were sold when she left Kenya in 1931 and some are in the MacMillan Library in Nairobi) but Universal Pictures donated some of the objects used in making the film and these are on display. Allow one hour to visit the museum and garden.

Turn left out of the museum on to Karen Road then left at the crossroads on to Langata Road and drive for 1½ km (1 mile) to the roundabout. Park at the *dukas* (grocery store) on the left after the roundabout. Before lunch look at the beautifully-made handicrafts (including candelabras, wooden picture frames, hand blown glass, leather-work, wrought iron and verdigris) in Marco Polo and Siafu shops. Eat at the outside terrace of the **Horseman** restaurant (try their seafood and coconut soup) but ask to see their evening menu and look in the restaurant inside upstairs – you'll probably want to come back here for dinner.

After lunch drive back along Langata Road towards Nairobi. Go past the Ostrich Park, then turn left into Forest Edge Road for the **Bomas of Kenya**. Aim to arrive by 2pm – it's less than 15 minutes from the Horseman. Watch their display of traditional dancing and visit the huts and see the handicrafts of some of Kenya's principal ethnic groups.

To return to Nairobi at the end of the day, drive back to Langata Road and turn right.

Dancing Bomas

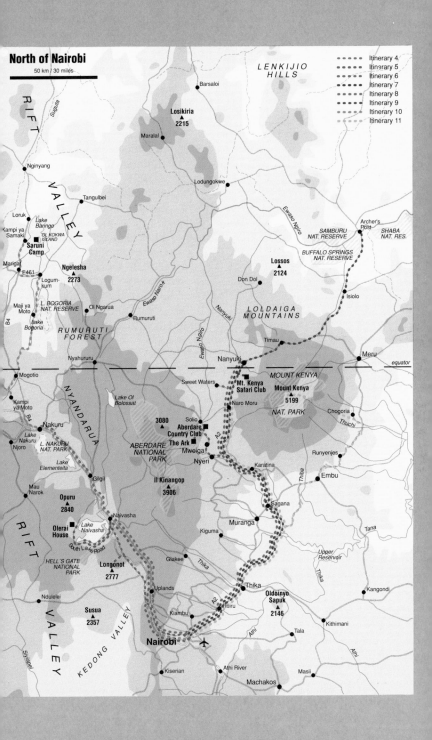

North of Nairobi

50 km / 30 miles

Itinerary 4
Itinerary 5
Itinerary 6
Itinerary 7
Itinerary 8
Itinerary 9
Itinerary 10
Itinerary 11

LENKIJIO HILLS

Barsaloi

Losikiria
2215

Maralal

Nginyang

Lodungokwe

RIFT

Tangulbei

Ewaso Ngiro

Archer's Post

SAMBURU NAT. RESERVE

SHABA NAT. RES.

Loruk

VALLEY

Lake Baringo

OL KOKWA ISLAND

Saruni Camp

BUFFALO SPRINGS NAT. RESERVE

Kampi ya Samaki

Lossos
2124

Marigat

E461

Ngelesha
2273

Logum-kum

Don Dol

Isiolo

Ewaso Narok

LOLDAIGA MOUNTAINS

Maji ya Moto

L. BOGORIA NAT. RESERVE

Ol Ngarua

Rumuruti

Nanyuki

B4

Lake Bogoria

RUMURUTI FOREST

Ewaso Njiro

Timau

Meru

equator

Nyahururu

Nanyuki

Mogotio

MOUNT KENYA

Sweet Waters

Mt. Kenya Safari Club

Mount Kenya
5199

Kampi ya Moto

NYANDARUA

Lake Ol Bolossat

Naro Moru

NAT. PARK

Chogoria

Thuchi

Nakuru

B4

3080

Solio

Aberdare Country Club

The Ark

Runyenjes

L. NAKURU NAT. PARK

Lake Nakuru

Njoro

ABERDARE NATIONAL PARK

Mweiga

Nyeri

A2

Embu

Lake Elementeita

Karatina

Thiba

Gilgil

Il Kinangop
3906

Mau Narok

Opuru
2840

Sagana

Tana

Muranga

Naivasha

Kiguma

Upper Reservoir

Olerai House

Lake Naivasha

South Lake Road

RIFT

HELL'S GATE NATIONAL PARK

Longonot
2777

Glakee

Thika

Thika

Kangondi

Kithimani

Ndulelei

Uplands

Thika

Oldoinyo Sapuk
2146

VALLEY

Susua
2357

Kiambu

Ruiru

A2

Tala

Kithimani

KEDONG VALLEY

Nairobi

Athi

Athi

Syabei

Kiserian

Athi River

Masii

Machakos

4. To the Top of a Volcano

A morning excursion to Mount Longonot, including a climb to the volcano's top, views of the Rift Valley and lunch in Naivasha.

From the roundabout on Kenyatta Avenue turn right on to Uhuru Highway. Continue straight ahead, over three roundabouts and stop at the ABC Shopping Centre on the left to buy some fruit and chocolate to eat on the top of Longonot.

Continue to drive out of town along Waiyaki Way (A104). You'll see crafts and produce for sale on the side of the roads – sheepskin hats, wicker baskets, fruit and vegetables, soapstone carvings, live fish, etc. Turn left shortly after the viewpoint signposted at 2,438m (8,000ft), following the signs to **Longonot** and South Kinangop. Drive to the police station outside Longonot village. Leave your car here and ask for a guide.

Hats for sale

It takes about 2 hours to climb to the summit of Longonot, known to the Maasai as *Oloonong'ot* (steep-ridged mountain). At 2,776m (9,108ft), it is the highest Rift Valley volcano in Kenya. It takes another 3 hours to walk around the brim (walk anti-clockwise). Be careful because the path crumbles in places and there's a steep drop. Buffalo are said to live in the vegetation at the bottom of the crater, though how they got there, nobody knows.

Walk back down the mountain and drive back to the main road and on to Naivasha. Stop off after 1½km (1 mile) at the viewpoint over Longonot to see where you climbed. Drive on to Naivasha, through town, over the speed bumps to the T-junction, then turn left towards Hell's Gate National Park. Cross the railway track and then take the left turn to get on South Lake Road. Go around the lake to **Lake Naivasha Hotel** (Tel: 0311-20013; PO Box 15, Naivasha) for lunch.

Afterwards, return to Nairobi on the A104.

Mount Longonot

5. Lake Naivasha and Crater Lake Sanctuary

An overnight trip to Lake Naivasha – with its beautiful views over the Rift Valley – and Crater Lake Sanctuary with its teeming wildlife. Dinner in an art deco house (black tie optional) and an ox-wagon safari on day two. See map on page 27.

–Book your ox-wagon safari when you book your accommodation–

Set off early to arrive in Naivasha mid-morning. To begin with, follow Itinerary 4 but don't turn off for Longonot. Drive past the first view point over the Rift Valley at 2,438m (8,000ft) – it's signposted – and stop at the second, on the left after the Kobil petrol station. You get a much better view from here and you won't be so hassled by souvenir sellers. At this point the land drops down to the valley floor with breathtaking views of mounts **Longonot** and **Susua** and **Lake Naivasha**. (See Itinerary 4 for directions on climbing Mount Longonot.)

Colobus monkey

From here, the road steeply descends to Lake Naivasha, still 45 minutes away. Turn left at the signposted junction, then drive through Naivasha town, over the speed bumps, to the crossroads. Turn left towards Hell's Gate National Park. Cross the railway track and then take the left turn to get on South Lake Road. Drive around the lake to **Olerai House** (Tel: 02-334868/891673 or 0311-30116; PO Box 54667, Nairobi; Fax: Nairobi 332106). The last 13km (8 miles) are dirt road. Spend the night here.

Olerai was the childhood home of Oria Douglas-Hamilton who, with her husband, Iain, is well-known in Kenya for conservation work, particularly with elephants. After lunch in the garden, visit **Crater Lake Sanctuary** and walk along the rim. You'll see colobus monkey, zebra, Thomson's gazelles, waterbuck and all types of birds. Relax back at Olerai House before changing for dinner over at Sirocco House, now the Douglas-Hamilton family home, built in the 1930 and a fine example of art deco architecture.

Next morning, walk along the Ndabibi Escarpment and have breakfast out in the bush. Later, go on an ox-wagon safari (best booked when you reserve your accommodation) across the plains for lunch or, for the less energetic, choose one of the options listed on the following page. Afterwards, you can drive back to Nairobi in the afternoon.

29

Cliffs in Hell's Gate National Park

Options for the second day:

•Sailing, boating, bird-watching, waterskiing, windsurfing and fishing can also be arranged through Oria Douglas-Hamilton.

•**Elsamere Conservation Centre near Crescent Island**: Watch a film of the life of the late Joy Adamson who raised Elsa, the orphan lion cub, and later released her back to the wild (a story made famous in the book and film *Born Free*). Have tea on the lawn of her home (daily: 3–6pm). All proceeds go to wildlife conservation. To contact the centre in advance, Tel: 0311-30079 or write to PO Box 1497, Naivasha.

•**Hell's Gate National Park**: This park, which gets its name from its steaming hot springs, contains East Africa's largest geothermal plant and is one of the rare parks where you are allowed to walk or cycle. There is plenty of game, including lions and leopards. The entrance to the park is off South Lake Road and is well signposted.

•**Elementeita Weavers**: Watch beautiful cotton and wool fabrics being hand-woven and buy carved wooden birds, ceramics, cushions, bedspreads, tablecloths, napkins, etc, from their shop. To find them, drive along South Lake Road, on the right about 200m (650ft) after the turn-off for Lake Naivasha Club.

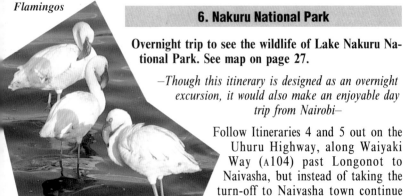

Flamingos

6. Nakuru National Park

Overnight trip to see the wildlife of Lake Nakuru National Park. See map on page 27.

–Though this itinerary is designed as an overnight excursion, it would also make an enjoyable day trip from Nairobi–

Follow Itineraries 4 and 5 out on the Uhuru Highway, along Waiyaki Way (A104) past Longonot to Naivasha, but instead of taking the turn-off to Naivasha town continue straight along on the A104. Nakuru is

REPUBLIC OF KENYA
NATIONAL PARKS

an hour's drive – 67km (42 miles) – further to the north. You'll pass Lake Elementeita before arriving in Nakuru, which in the Maasai language means *dust bowl*.

Lake Nakuru is famous for its flamingos which from a distance appear like pink icing over the lake. There are also pelicans, storks and numerous other bird species, as well as lion, leopard, bushbuck, waterbuck, impala, gazelles, rhino, monkeys, baboons and hippo (the latter are best seen at sunset when they yawn, snort and climb out of the mud on to the shore to graze). There are also over 120 Rothschild's giraffes in the park, which is the best place to find this unusual species.

This is a well-maintained and easily accessible game park, well suited to anyone used to the rigours of driving in typical Kenya bush country. It takes 2 hours to drive around the lake. Don't miss the euphorbia (candelabra) trees on the west side, the largest euphorbia forest in East Africa. Look out for rhino in the grasslands in the south and the two white rhino in the southeast, which you'll be lucky to see.

Drive down to the lake shore (mud and season permitting) and get out of your vehicle for a closer look at the birds. Then drive up to **Baboon Cliffs** for a beautiful view down over the lake – which is particularly impressive when a storm is rolling up the Rift Valley. Watch that storm closely, however!

Stay the night at **Sarova Lion Hill Camp** (Tel: 02-333233; PO Box 30680, Nairobi; Telex 22223).

Next morning, endeavour to get up early and go on an early morning game drive before breakfast. Watch the birds waking up, preening and eating, and see the hippos returning to the water after their night's grazing.

Set off back to Nairobi in the early afternoon, aiming to arrive in the city before dusk.

It's a hippo's life!

Overnight trip to Nanyuki and Mount Kenya Safari Club, waking early on day two for a pre-dawn ride through Mount Kenya Game Ranch. See map on page 27.

–Mount Kenya Safari Club is 205km (127 miles) or about 2½ hours from Nairobi and makes a very relaxing overnight excursion. It can also be combined with a trip to the superbly-located Ark (Itinerary 8) and with trips further north to Isiolo and Samburu (Itinerary 9) or Lewa Downs and Maralal (Itinerary 15) and Turkana (Itinerary 16)–

From Uhuru Highway drive along Kenyatta Avenue and turn left on to Moi Avenue. Turn right at the signs for UN Environment Programme/Gigiri and then follow the road down to the round-

Across the equator

about. Go straight ahead up the hill and continue straight over the next four roundabouts, following signs for the A2 to Thika. This road bypasses Kahawa Army barracks, Thika town, and goes through Karatina, 128km (80 miles) away. It is good tarmac all the way except for one pot-holed patch stretching between 44 and 56km (27–35 miles) out of Nairobi.

This very fertile region is settled with predominantly Kikuyu smallholdings and was the heartland of the *Mau Mau* rebellion that eventually led to Kenyan independence (see *History & Culture*).

The turn-off to the right for Nanyuki is at the bottom of a curving hill, 13km (8 miles) after Karatina, and is clearly sign-posted to the Aberdare Country Club, Naro Moro River Lodge and Mountain Lodge.

Mount Kenya Safari Club (Tel: 02-216940; PO Box 58581, Nairobi; Fax: 02-216796; Telex: 22066) is also well-signposted and is 64km (40 miles) from this turn-off, just after the second equator crossing (the first equator you will traverse is a fake – the invention of souvenir touts).

After checking in, book tomorrow's pre-breakfast horse ride at the reception and then wander (or jog) around the 36 hectares (90 acres) of beautiful grounds, complete with sacred ibis, Egyptian geese, yellow-billed storks, peacocks and ornamental ponds, or swim in the only heated swimming-pool on the equator. You can also play golf, tennis, bowls, croquet or snooker, go fishing, bird-watching or mountain-climbing, or use the health and beauty centre. There's also an art gallery (very expensive) with some magnificent exhibits, and a resident artist, Vitalis Ochieng Oduo, who paints portraits and pictures of Africa in what used to be the exercise room located under the swimming-pool.

Pool at the Safari Club

After lunch, visit the **animal orphanage**, set up as a study area for Kenyan school children to see Kenya's only captive breeding herd of bongo. Other animals include a chimpanzee, Max, who was rescued from poachers in the Congo, monkeys, cheetah, gazelles, zebras and other orphaned or wounded animals that need medical care before they can be rehabilitated to the wild.

Relax before dressing for the seven-course dinner – this is one of the few Kenyan restaurants where men must wear jacket and tie (women should also dress smartly).

Next morning, ride before breakfast. On horseback is the best way to approach most African game, because the latter cannot smell you or recognise your silhouette as that of a human when you are in the saddle. Ask to explore the 485 hectares (1,200 acres) of bushland that have been transformed into Mount Kenya Game Ranch (not actually part of the Safari Club – but the latter should be able to request access for you).

Before setting off back to Nairobi, visit **Nanyuki Spinners and Weavers** (Tel: Nanyuki 22251; PO Box 25, Nanyuki; open Monday-Friday 9am–5pm; Saturday 9am–1pm). This women's cooperative makes beautiful hand-spun, hand-woven rugs, shawls and blankets coloured with locally-produced natural plant dyes. To watch the women at work, drive back to the A2 and turn right and drive along Meru Road through Nanyuki town. Turn left on to the C76 at Kenya Commercial Bank. The workshops are 1km (½ mile) along this road on the left, opposite the District Hospital.

The animal orphanage

A two-night trip to Aberdare National Park, a region famous for its lions, and Sweet Waters Tented Camp, with log fires, floodlit water-holes, waterfalls and flame trees. See map on page 27.

Follow Itinerary 7 as far as Karatina. Don't take the turn-off for Nanyuki – in spite of the sign saying Aberdare Country Club. Instead, continue straight ahead and into Nyeri town. Drive through Nyeri town towards Mweiga. Follow the signs to the Aberdare Country Club up a dirt road on the right.

View from the Ark

The **Aberdare Country Club** (Tel: 0171 55620 or Nairobi 216940; PO Box 449, Nyeri or Lonrho Hotels Ltd, PO Box 58581, Nairobi; Fax: Nairobi 216796; Telex: 22066) was once a watering-hole for early white settlers and is now a luxurious lodge/hotel with a nine-hole golf course, riding, fishing, tennis, magnificent views of Mount Kenya and a wildlife sanctuary to walk in. It's a popular overnight weekend haunt for the expatriate community.

The **Aberdares** are a steep volcanic massif covered in moorland and dense forest (some of the oldest trees in the country) to the west of Mount Kenya. This beautiful but wild region is home to some of the fiercest lions in Kenya and it is where man-eaters are dumped from other game parks when they are caught. Black leopard, serval cat and other melanistic (dark-coloured) animals also live here. There is excellent trout-fishing in the high mountain streams and several impressive waterfalls.

Aberdare National Park is not easy to visit because the dirt roads are inaccessible in heavy rains (and it rains a lot) and the thick forest makes game viewing difficult. However, you are staying at **The Ark**, also owned by Lonrho and built like Noah's vessel in a sea of trees – they even pull in the drawbridge at night. (Transport is provided from the Aberdare Country Club to the Ark, leaving at 2.30pm and arriving at the Ark about 45 minutes later after a short drive through the game park.) The flood-lit salt lick and water-hole attract elephants, rhino, lion, gazelle, antelope and numerous other animals, particularly after dark.

Watch from the comfort of the glass-walled bar with roaring log fire (it gets very cold at night) or go down into the lookout hide close to the water-hole. This has open window slits so that you can not only see every whisker but also smell the elephant and buffalo a few metres away. The resident game warden (yes, they call him Noah) keeps watch at night and will awaken you if he sights anything unusual in the small hours. Children under 8 years old are not allowed to stay here.

Stay overnight at the Ark and then return to Aberdare Country Club in time for lunch the next day.

Having eaten your fill, drive to **Sweet Waters Tented Camp** (Tel: 0171-55620; PO Box 763, Nairobi; Fax: 0171-23414) a few kilometres outside **Nanyuki**. Turn left out of the Aberdare Country Club and follow the dirt road to the main tarmac road. Turn left and drive towards Nanyuki. The turn-off for Sweet Waters is a few kilometres before town on the left, opposite the Silverbeck Hotel, just after the first equator. It's 15km (9 miles) from here to the camp.

The land used to belong to Adnan Kashoggi, the arms dealer, but was taken over by Lonrho in settlement of debts. The luxurious safari tents (with bathroom and bidet) enjoy incredible views of Mount Kenya and over-

Family group

look a water-hole frequented by elephants and other game. At sundown and sunrise the next morning game drive around the private ranch. Be sure to visit the resident tame rhino (scratch his horn!).

Arrange to visit **Solio Ranch** (Tel: Nairobi 02 763638; PO Box 30595, Nairobi – or via Aberdare Country Club, which has a special arrangement with Solio) after breakfast next day. This private ranch set in thorn-scrub and open grassland is now a rhino sanctuary and has been very successful in reintroducing rhinos to the wild. You will also see oryx, eland, leopard, giraffe and colobus monkeys. To get there, take the road to Mweiga from Nanyuki. Drive for about 8km (5 miles) and turn right at the signs for Solio Ranch, just after the big dip.

Return to Nairobi before nightfall via Nyeri and **Thika** (allow 2½ hours). Stop off at the Blue Posts Inn just before Thika to visit the waterfalls and admire the flame trees made famous in Elspeth Huxley's novel *The Flame Trees of Thika*.

Sweet Waters

9. Samburu and Shaba

A two-night excursion to Samburu and Shaba National Reserves, stopping en route to see traditional craftsmen at work. Staying the first night at Larsen's Camp in Samburu and rising early to explore Buffalo Springs, and spending the second night at Shaba, where Joy Adamson rehabilitated leopards. See map on page 27.

This is my favourite part of Kenya and, after the Masai Mara, it is the first place I take visitors.

Buy the Survey of Kenya map of Samburu and Buffalo Springs National Reserves. Aim to set off by 8.30am and you will be in Samburu by lunchtime. Follow Itinerary 7 as far as Nanyuki. Drive straight through town and continue along the A2 through Timau to **Isiolo** – it's about 300km (186 miles) or 3½ hours on good tarmac roads from Nairobi.

Isiolo is the frontier town bordering the wilds of northern Kenya. A crossroads for Samburu, Somalis, Asians, Rendille, Boran and Turkana peoples, it's a great place to people-watch. Wander around the colourful market on the left just before the mosque at the beginning of town. Bargain with the local youths for souvenirs, including beaten steel, copper and brass bangles, and Somali daggers in intricately decorated leather sheaths. These vendors can be very persistent so be polite but firm or you'll find yourself loaded with trinkets you don't really want. For a few shillings, they will take you behind the bushes at the back of the market to see the craftsmen at work – huddled over outdoor fires heated white-hot with foot-pumped bellows made of a goat's stomach, or hammering the semi-molten metal on improvised anvils.

Before leaving Isiolo, fill up with petrol at one of the garages about 300m (⅕ mile) further down the A2 into town. Then keep driving straight until you get to the police check-point where you must register your vehicle and number of passengers. Continue north, bearing left on the main road 100 metres after the barrier. Beyond this point is very wild and barren – just acacia scrubland with few other bushes. It is very dusty in the dry season.

All together now…

Samburu women

You're now on the main road to both Samburu and Shaba National Reserves, about 45km (28 miles) or an hour away. The tarmac ends at Isiolo and, from there on, the dirt roads are heavily 'corrugated' which can be a bit rough and bouncy. Grit your teeth and drive as fast as you dare – at least 70km (43 miles) per hour – it's more comfortable this way, though it won't do your vehicle much good. Inside the reserves, the road is usually smoother (although still dirt) and the wildlife more than make up for any small aches!

Cross over the Ewaso Ngiro River, drive into Archer's Post village where you turn left – it's well signposted – to enter **Samburu** by the Archer's Post Gate. Then you can enjoy a game drive to Larsen's Camp (Tel: 02-335807; PO Box 47557, Nairobi; Fax: 02-340541; Telex: 22146 BLOCOTELS) where you're staying the night. In particular, look out for blue-legged Somali ostrich, Grevy's zebra, leopard, elephant, reticulated giraffe, oryx, cheetah and puff adder on the way.

After a late lunch, a siesta and tea, game drive west along the river. Drive back to Samburu Game Lodge in time for the leopard baiting at sundown and to see the crocodiles fed. It's close to **Larsen's Camp** so you can drive back there before dark.

Before breakfast next day, cross over the river and game drive in **Buffalo Springs National Reserve** which adjoins Samburu. Follow the road east along the river to get to the **Buffalo Springs** which were apparently blasted out of the ground when an Italian pilot dumped his bombs in the reserve during World War II. Exit Samburu by the Buffalo Springs Gate and turn left on to the A2 to Marsabit. Drive a little way north, towards Archer's Post and then turn right at the signposts for Shaba Sarova Lodge.

Like Samburu, **Shaba National Reserve** is on the banks of the Ewaso Ngiro (Black River), whose riverine swamp attracts elephant and other game. More remote and less visited than Samburu, this is the reserve where the late Joy Adamson rehabilitated leopards to the wild. Stay the night at **Sarova Shaba** (Tel: 02-333248/9/50; PO Box 30680, Nairobi; Fax: 02-211472; Telex: 22223 SAROVA KE).

Leave Shaba by 2pm at the latest next day to get back to Nairobi by nightfall.

Archer's Post

Something stirring in Lake Baringo sunset

10. Three Lakes

Three-day trip to Lake Nakuru (flamingos and pelicans), Lake Bogoria (hot springs and geysers), and Lake Baringo (hippos, crocodiles, bird walks and boating). See map on page 27.

—You'll be driving on both tarmac and some quite rough dirt roads so a four-wheel-drive vehicle is essential for this itinerary. Note: my recommendation for overnight accommodation, Lake Baringo Saruni Cam, is not suitable for families with small children as the island rises steeply out of the water and there are no fences to prevent children falling. Families are advised to stay at Lake Baringo Club on the mainland—

On day one of this itinerary, follow Itinerary 6 to Lake Nakuru, staying at Sarova Lion Hill Camp (Tel: 02-333233). Before going to sleep, order a picnic lunch box to take with you next day. In the morning, game drive in the park before breakfast, then drive back through the main park gate along Flamingo and Moi roads to Nakuru town. Turn left on to Kenyatta Avenue and follow signs for the B4, signposted to Marigat. Pass through Kampi ya Moto and turn right at Mogotio on to the dirt road signposted to **Lake Bogoria National Reserve**.

Pelican on Lake Nakuru

Lake Bogoria is a shallow soda lake at the foot of the sheer-faced Laikipia Escarpment. The landscape is burnt and rocky and seemingly inhospitable to wildlife. However, often there are sometimes more flamingos here than at Lake Nakuru further south, though this depends on the depth of water and the amount of algae it contains. There are also hundreds of birds and some game, including the usual gazelle, impala, etc. At the southern end of the reserve you may see klipspringers and greater kudu.

You are taking a back route to the lake but apart from a few stony patches, the road is well-graded. On leaving Mogotio, for the next 24km (15 miles) you drive along-side sisal (spiky cactus) plantations as far as Mugurin. Drive straight on for 20km (12 miles) from Mugurin and turn right at Maji ya Moto to enter the reserve by the western Majimoto Gate. Drive down towards the lake and take the left fork to get to the **hot springs**. Here, get out of your car and walk down to the water's edge to watch the geysers – but be careful: many visitors have been burned by the hot jets.

On leaving the hot springs turn left and drive to the southern end of the park. Look out for klipspringers and greater kudu here. Retrace your route past the hot springs and exit the reserve by the northern Loboi Gate. Before leaving, follow the smaller tracks down to the flat lake bed, turn off your engine and get out and walk around. It's the best way to appreciate the silence and heat.

Fish from Lake Baringo

Once out of the reserve, drive 21km (13 miles) along the E461 dirt road to the tarmacked B4 road from Nakuru to Loruk. Turn right (this junction is signposted) and continue through Marigat to the junction on the right leading to **Kampi ya Samaki**, 123km (76 miles) after Nakuru. There's a garage on the corner. Drive another 3km (2 miles), turning left after Lake Baringo Club (ornithologists should call in to arrange a bird walk along the cliffs for the following afternoon). Follow the dirt road through Kampi ya Samaki village (ask for directions if you can't find the signposts). Drive to the end then follow the track down towards the lake. Park your car here, remembering to take all valuables with you, then walk down to the jetty and wait to be whisked across the water in a shallow dingy on the 20-minute trip to **Lake Baringo Saruni Camp** on Ol Kokwa Island (Tel: 02-333285 or 212370/1/2;

Chartered Expeditions Kenya Ltd/Utali Tours and Safaris Ltd, PO Box 61542, Nairobi; Fax: 02-228875; Telex: 22992).

The freshwater Lake Baringo is one of the most northern of the Rift Valley lakes and is home to crocodiles, hippos and over 450 species of birds. The water looks permanently muddy due to its chemical composition which keeps silt particles circulating and stops them sinking to the bottom. Often, and always just before dawn, the lake is as still as the proverbial glass, but when a storm rolls over the valley, the water churns with waves several metres high. Despite the crocodiles, you can water-ski and swim, albeit at your own risk. The volcanic scenery is dramatically beautiful.

Once on Ol Kokwa Island, you can swim in the pool, sit and watch the lake, take a guided bird walk or water-ski, or simply relax after the drive. Accommodation is in luxury tents each with its own bird feeder. To unwind fully, stay here two nights.

Book the pre-breakfast boating trip across the lake and up the **Molo River** – it's very beautiful, with hippo, heron and numerous other water birds en route. Arrange to see the village of the local Njemps people.

Return to Nairobi via Nakuru and Naivasha – even with a pause for sodas the city is just over 4 hours away.

11. Mount Kenya

A five-day trek from east to west across Mount Kenya. See map on page 27.

—Camping stoves, boots, waterproofs, tents, balaclavas, torches, etc, can be hired from Naro Moru River Lodge (Tel: 0171-22018/22548; PO Box 18, Naro Moru) or from Natural Action Treks (Tel/Fax: 02-740214; PO Box 12516, Nairobi) in the Museum Hill Shopping Centre opposite the museum (see Itinerary 1). They can also fix up guides and other walking itineraries. Ask for Sammy Kariuk—

You don't have to be a mountaineer to cross Mount Kenya (5,199m/17,057ft) but it's a stiff walk and you need to be properly equipped and pretty fit. Ideally, you should also have experienced climbing at this height before, to know how your body will react. Inevitably the clouds roll down from the mountain-top around lunchtime and it rains or snows almost every day, even in the dry season. Don't even think of climbing without a warm sleeping-bag, woollen gloves, scarf and hat, and proper walking boots. And remember to take all your own food as there are no shops or restaurants en route.

'Everlasting flowers' on Kenya's mountains

Be prepared!

On the way, watch your step, but also look out for buffalo, elephant, malachite sunbirds, eagles, rock hyrax, bottle brush flowers, giant lobelia, groundsel and alpine heather.

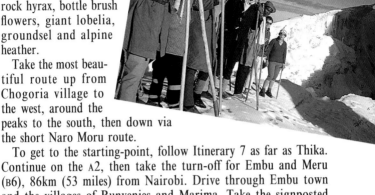

Take the most beautiful route up from Chogoria village to the west, around the peaks to the south, then down via the short Naro Moru route.

To get to the starting-point, follow Itinerary 7 as far as Thika. Continue on the A2, then take the turn-off for Embu and Meru (B6), 86km (53 miles) from Nairobi. Drive through Embu town and the villages of Runyenjes and Marima. Take the signposted turn-off to Kiangoji (D474), 3km (2 miles) after Marima on the left.

Drive for 3km (2 miles) past the Chogoria Transit Hotel and turn left at the Mukutano Bar and Restaurant. Drive for 4km (2½ miles) past the shops and turn right. Chogoria Forest Station is 1km (¾ mile) down this road.

The park entrance is 21km (13 miles) higher up at 2,990m (9,810ft). The road passes through mountain forest and, in a series of hairpin bends, up to the bamboo zone. Spend the night at **Meru Mount Kenya Bandas** (take the right turn-off ½km/¼ mile before the gate entrance on the right). Ask to stay in the cottage when you book (Tel: Let's Go Travel Ltd, 02-340331/213033; PO Box 60342, Nairobi; Fax: 02-336890; Telex: c/o 25440 Brusafari). You can arrange for guides and porters to carry your bags up the mountain at Natural Action Ltd's shop up at the bandas. If you have a driver, tell him to pick you up at the Naro Moru park entrance in four days' time. If you don't have a driver, arrange for transport back to your car with Natural Action Ltd.

Set out early next morning on the 5-hour walk to **Minto's Hut**. The path crosses over a stream and then follows the ridge and is well marked. The views down to the Gorges Valley are superb. Remember to take water with you as there are no fresh sources en route.

On the third day walk to **Austrian Hut**, at the foot of Point Lenana. The route leads up the valley, across scree slopes,

Mountain Sickness

More people die of pulmonary oedema on Mount Kenya each year than on any other mountain. It is caused by an accumulation of water on the lungs or brain. The symptoms are headaches, nausea, sleeplessness, loss of appetite, swelling and fluid retention, slurred speech and abnormal behaviour. The only cure is to get to a lower altitude – as quickly as possible. To avoid pulmonary oedema, allow time to get accustomed to the altitude before going higher up.

Camping out

and (very steeply) up to Square Tarn. From here, continue straight on to the col below Point Lenana, descend for a short way, then continue over another scree slope before reaching Austrian Hut. You should spend the night here.

Set off at 4.30am the next morning to climb to **Point Lenana**, a steep 1½-hour scramble. There's only one way, so you can't get lost. Take only chocolate and water with you – leave the rest of your baggage with the porters. You'll be at the top of the mountain at dawn when the views are clearest and you'll feel exhilarated that you've climbed the second highest mountain in Africa.

Come down to breakfast at Austrian Hut and then descend the steep scree slope to **Mackinders Hut** on the west side of the mountain, about 1½ hours away. Spend the day pottering around here.

Next morning, walk down through the vertical bog – set at a 45° angle and streaming with rivulets of water all through the year – across open moorland and down through the forest to the Meteo-

rological Station. From here it's only 9km (5 miles) to the park entrance where your driver will hopefully be waiting to take you to Naro Moru River Lodge for refreshments and a celebratory drink. (If you set off early and have enough energy, you can walk from Lenana to Naro Moru in one day, although this is very tiring and by the end your knees will be trembling).

You can easily drive back to Nairobi the same day. From Naro Moru River Lodge drive back to the main A2 road and turn right. Nairobi is 171km (106 miles) or about 2¼ hours away.

View from the top

A day trip to see the birdlife of Lake Magadi, with magnificent views of the Ngong Hills and Rift Valley and a visit to Olorgasailie prehistoric site en route. This is one of the hottest, least populated places in Kenya, so take a jerry-can of water, extra fuel and travel only in a reliable vehicle. Don't forget your sunglasses, sunhat and sun-cream and take a picnic lunch.

Over the Ngong to Magadi

Order your picnic lunch the day before departing from Pasara (2nd Floor, Lonrho House on Standard Street; Tel: 02-338247; open Monday to Friday 9am–5pm and Saturday 9am–2pm).

From Kenyatta Avenue, drive left along Uhuru Highway to the third roundabout. Turn right on to Langata Road and drive out past Nairobi National Park to Magadi Road (c58), on the left. Turn here and keep driving straight, through Ongata Rongai, and up the southeast flank of the Ngong Hills at 2,135m (7,005ft). After 32km (20 miles) from Nairobi, the ground drops dramatically to the Rift Valley floor below and the wind whistles up the cliff face. Follow the dirt road on the left to the viewpoint.

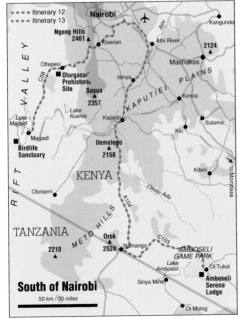

This is the vista that is said to have inspired Isak Dinesen to write *Out of Africa.*

Continue on the c58 down the hairpin bends of the escarpment towards the heat. Just after the tiny village of Oltepesi take the signposted left turn to **Olorgasailie Prehistoric Site**, 1½km (1 mile) away, where one of our earliest ancestors, *Homo erectus,* killed a group of giant baboon-like creatures using crude stone flints and left their remains and weapons to be discovered by Dr Louis

43

Leakey almost half a million years later. Spend an hour or so visiting the site with a resident guide from the National Museum. Then drive on to the pink and white waters of **Lake Magadi**, 45km (28 miles) further south through the Ol Keju Nyiro Valley.

The 100 sq-km (38 sq-mile) lake is only 580m (1,903ft) above sea level and is one of the richest sources of sodium sesquicarbonate or soda in the world.

Drive to the gate, where you register your vehicle. Then drive along the causeway and up to the T-junction. Turn right, then left and around the factory, keeping it on your left. Cross over another causeway and, after 1km (⅔ mile), take the smallest of the two tracks leading straight ahead (the main track, which you don't take, goes to the right). Drive over three more causeways, stopping off to feel the searing heat. The track then turns to the right and then, sharply, to the left. Leave your car at the bottom and walk up the track on the left to the viewpoint about ½ km (¼ mile) away. It is a steep climb but the view is well worth it.

Leave in good time to retrace your route back to Nairobi before dark (allow at least 3½ hours).

13. Amboseli National Park

An overnight trip to see the wildlife of Amboseli National Park, against the backdrop of Mount Kilimanjaro, Africa's highest. See map on page 43.

—If you don't want to drive to Amboseli, you can fly from Wilson Airport in Nairobi or from Mombasa (see Practical Information*)—*

From Kenyatta Avenue turn left on to Uhuru Highway and drive straight on, over three roundabouts. Take the right fork for Athi

River after 24km (15 miles). You're now on the A104, heading through Isinya and Kajiado for Namanga and the Tanzanian border, 135km (84 miles) away. On a clear day, you'll be able to see the 5,895m (19,340ft), snowcapped Mount Kilimanjaro, the highest peak in Africa, for most of the journey.

From Namanga follow the signs to the C103 and

Mount Kilimanjaro

the entrance to the Amboseli National Park is 70km (43 miles) further on. This dirt road is heavily corrugated, and you might find the drive rather tiring.

Amboseli has no shortage of elephants

As you continue through the park you'll see the shimmering mirage of dry **Lake Amboseli** (Maasai for 'salt dust') which fills up with water only very occasionally in the rainy season. You'll also see plenty of dead and dying trees – killed by saline volcanic salts in the underground water and by hordes of foraging elephants. There are hundreds of elephants in the freshwater swamps in the southeast. In fact far too many for this tiny 392 sq-km (152 sq-mile) park and they are partly to blame for the environmental destruction. Tourist vehicles driving off-road are also responsible, so stick to the tracks, regardless of how close you would like to get to observe the wildlife.

But don't be put off by first impressions – Amboseli's charm will soon win you over. Be sure to watch the sun set (not directly) behind Kilimanjaro and look out for Maasai *moran* people watering their cattle (be prepared to pay them if you want to take their pictures). You'll also see buffalo, gazelle, vultures, hyena, giraffe, baboon and maybe rhino and lion.

Maasai body painting

You should book to stay the night at the Amboseli Serena Lodge, (Tel: 02-725111; PO Box 46302, Nairobi; Fax: 02-725184; Telex: 22377). Then return to Nairobi the next morning.

A two-night trip to Masai Mara, including a balloon ride and a champagne breakfast. Luxury tented camp, beautiful scenery and the best wildlife in Kenya.

–Book your balloon safari before leaving Nairobi, along with your accommodation and transport for game viewing. Whom you book with depends on your departure point, which in turn depends on the time of year (see advice given in itinerary). Note: it is also possible to fly to the Mara twice daily from Wilson Airport; the flight takes 45 minutes–

Buy the Macmillan map of the Masai Mara in Nairobi (available at most bookshops and hotels). It shows the major tracks and will give you some sense of direction in this 1,530 sq-km (590 sq-miles) reserve. The best time to go is in July and August when millions of

Shop near Narok

wildebeest and other plains game migrate into the Mara in search of grazing from the Serengeti National Park in Tanzania. At any time of year you are more likely to see the big five – lion, buffalo, elephant, leopard and rhino – than in any other reserve.

When you book your balloon safari ask in advance about weather conditions in the Mara so that you can decide where to take off from, as this varies according to the time of year (you'll understand why later in this itinerary).

Follow Itinerary 2 as far as Ruaka. Instead of turning right, drive straight on. Don't turn off on to the new road to Naivasha and Nakuru. You're now on the B3, the old road to Naivasha, which winds down the Rift Valley escarpment and offers beautiful views over the valley floor and mountains Susua and Longonot. Buy a bag of plums from the sellers along the road side to eat on the journey. The tiny church nestling in the hillside towards the bottom of the escarpment was built by Italian prisoners of war during World War II. A few kilometres after the church turn left (but still on the B3) to Narok, 90km (56 miles) away. The first 25km (15 miles) or so are riddled with potholes but the road improves shortly after you pass the satellite dishes.

Narok is the capital of Maasai country and is the last place where you can refuel before reaching the reserve. Avoid the souvenir-sellers by driving through town and stopping at the first garage out-

The Annual Migration

In April, about 1.6 million wildebeest gather on the Serengeti plains in Tanzania and prepare to journey north, following the rains, in search of new grazing and water. They are accompanied on their journey by zebra and gazelles. Towards the beginning of July the enormous herds reach the Masai Mara and then spread out across the plains to forage for sustenance. Once the plains are grazed dry the animals move on, crossing north out of the Mara in the east of the reserve and between the Mara and Talek rivers. Only the strongest survive the long treks north and south. Weak animals either die of fatigue, drown in rivers or are hunted by predators such as lion, leopard or cheetah. Towards mid-September the herds begin to gather in preparation for the crossing back into the Tanzanian plains where they arrive towards the end of December. Young are born in February and March in the Serengeti.

side Narok on the right at the top of the hill. You can also buy cold sodas, snacks and souvenirs here. After Narok drive straight for 20km (13 miles) until you reach Ewaso Ngiro where you cross the river with the same name.

In the rainy season (generally from the end of March to the beginning of June and mid-October to mid-December, but always check current weather conditions) turn left at Ewaso Ngiro on to the tarmacked c12. This road becomes dirt after another 55km (34 miles) and leads to the east of the reserve, entering via the Sekenani Gate (about 4 hours from Nairobi).

Stay at **Keekorok Lodge** (Tel: 02-335807; Block Hotels, PO Box 47557, Nairobi; Fax: 02-340541; Telex: 22146 BLOCOTELS), 23km (14 miles) from Sekenani Gate, which is always surrounded by

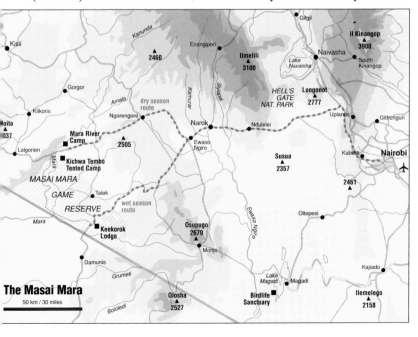

The Masai Mara
50 km / 30 miles

plenty of wildlife. If visiting in the rainy season book your balloon safari from here.

If conditions are dry, from Ewaso Ngiro go straight along the dirt road (c13), turn on to the E176 (also a dirt road) and enter the reserve via the Ololoolo Gate to the west. This takes about 5½ hours from Nairobi. Stay at **Mara River Camp** (Tel: 02-331191 or 229009; PO Box 48019, Nairobi) or at **Kichwa Tembo Tented Camp** (Tel 02-217497/336805: Windsor Hotels International, PO Box 74957, Nairobi; Fax: 02-217498; Telex: 25182 WINDSO), just outside the reserve. Be warned, though – it is no joke to be bogged down in the black cotton soil and in wet conditions you may be stranded for some time, so avoid this area in the rainy season.

Dry-season travellers should book their balloon safari from Little Governor's Camp (Tel: 02-331871/2 or 02-331041; Musiara Ltd, PO Box 48217, Nairobi).

Best view of the Masai

It's impossible to be specific about where you'll see the various animals but, generally speaking, look for lion hunting close to bushes on the plains at dusk or sunrise; cheetah sitting astride rocks on the open Burrungat plains; leopard in riverine forest; elephant near rivers and in swampy areas; and rhino in scrubby bush country (near the Burrungat plains). Buffalo are everywhere, as are the various gazelles and antelopes, zebra, giraffe, warthog, topi, etc. There are several hippo pools along the Mara River which bisects the reserve from north to south. Visit hippo at dusk when they stop wallowing in the mud and clamber out to graze. But stay in your vehicle if they're out of the water and never block their access to the river – more tourists are killed by hippo than any other mammal, with crocodile claiming most victims overall. Avoid the hippo pool at the Tanzanian border after 4pm as tourist vehicles

Masai meeting

have been known to be at-
tacked by bandits who then
flee across the border at sundown to avoid arrest by the
Kenyan authorities.

Early next morning take
a balloon safari (we went
up one Christmas dawn
wearing black tie and
ball-gowns). Take a hat
to protect your head from
the heat of the burner. Spend a hour or so
drifting above the animals (marvellous photo opportuni-
ties) then land and enjoy a champagne breakfast out in the bush.
This will undoubtedly be a highlight of your holiday and is well
worth the expense (around US$320).

You'll be driven back to your vehicle and can spend the rest of
the day game driving or resting at camp.

15. Four-night Safari

To Lewa Downs (horse-riding among game), Samburu (elephant, cheetah, leopard), Maralal (buffalo, gazelle, warthog, Grevy zebra, reticulated giraffe, impala, eland and hyena), Lake Baringo (crocodile, hippo), Lake Bogoria (greater kudu and klipspringer) and Nakuru (flamingos and baboon).

—This itinerary covers virtually the same ground as Itinerary 16, but focuses on different attractions and takes less time—

Follow Itinerary 7 as far as Nanyuki. Drive through Nanyuki town
and continue on the A2 through Timau, then take the left turn
which is signposted to Isiolo. Look out for the painted oil drums
on the left signposting the entrance to Lewa Downs/Wilderness
Trails. It takes about 30 minutes to drive
from the tarmac road to the ranch-house.

Lewa Downs is one of the best places to
stay in Kenya. It is a private ranch owned
and run by the Craig family who can tell
you everything you want to know about
the country. Accommodation is in one
of six cottages where a maximum of
12 visitors can stay at a time, and
meals are eaten *en famille*. Try to
do everything on offer, including
the day and night game drives,
guided game and bird walks, a visit
to the orphaned baby elephant and
the rug weavers and spinners and,

Cheetah

best of all, the horse-back ride among the game. Arrange to do this next morning before breakfast – it's the best way to get close to wildlife, particularly giraffe, as they can't recognise your smell or shape on horseback.

On the second day drive out of Lewa Downs after lunch and back on to the main road to Isiolo. Continue as for Itinerary 9 and aim to spend the night at **Samburu National Reserve.**

On the third morning, start with a game drive through the reserve and then leave it by the West Gate.

Maralal is about 180km (112 miles) or a day's drive away, along dirt roads through beautiful and seldom-visited countryside. There are few signposts so keep driving straight on what looks like the main track and ask everyone you see if you're going in the right direction (just point and say the name of the town you're heading for very clearly). You'll pass first through Ngotogongoron, then Barsalinga, and shortly afterwards you will come to a T-junction where the track joins up with the C78 from Isiolo. Turn left to get to Lodungokwe and then follow the signs to Kisima, 57km (36 miles) from the T-junction and Maralal, 19km (11 miles) further. En route you'll see buffalo, gazelle, warthog, Grevy zebra (fine stripes, rounded 'teddy-bear' ears and white underbelly), reticulated giraffe, impala, eland and hyena.

Maralal nestles in the foothills of the Samburu Highlands and is the area's administrative headquarters. Many of the *Mau Mau* resistance leaders, including Kenyatta, were imprisoned here during the years leading up to independence (see *History*). The streets are very dusty and the nights are so cold that roaring log fires are not only welcoming but a necessity.

Main street, Maralal

Stay at the **Maralal Safari Lodge** (Tel: 0368-2060/2417; Thorn Tree Safaris, PO Box 42475, Nairobi; Fax: 0368-2299 – this is actually the number for the Kenya Commercial Bank but your fax will be passed on) on the outskirts of town on the way to Lake Turkana. Turn left at the first roundabout (on the corner with the police station), then drive straight across the second roundabout. The lodge is signposted from here. You'll be escorted to your cottage by the resident night watchman who makes sure that the buffalo which wander nightly out of the forest to graze around are not lurking ready to attack. Less threatening elephants, zebra and gazelle also wander close by.

The lodge's main attraction is the water-hole where buffalo and common zebra come to drink. Order a picnic lunch to take with you next day.

In the morning, wander around the market and persuade a Samburu *moran* to show you how to test the quality of the genuine Samburu spears and bows and arrows on sale. The Samburu are a semi-nomadic, cattle-rearing people, who are closely related to the more well-known Maasai.

Set off for Lake Baringo before midday. Go back the way you came along the c78 road towards Samburu National Reserve. At Kisima, turn right on to the c77 signposted Rumuruti and Loruk.

Shortly after Sukuta lol Marmar – 32km (20 miles) after Kisima – take the right fork for Tangulbei, 45km (28 miles) further on. Drive through the village and take the left fork to Loruk about 5km (3 miles) later.

This is a spectacular road across the Lerochi Plateau and down the northern end of **Lake Baringo**, where it joins the b4 to Nanyuki.

Stay the night at Lake Baringo, then return to Nairobi the next morning via **Lake Bogoria** and **Lake Nakuru** (see Itinerary 10 for the homeward bound route in reverse, and details of what to look out for on the way back).

Samburu warrior

On the shores of Lake Turkana

16. A Grand Tour to Lake Turkana

This is an action-packed seven-day trip to Lake Turkana, incorporating many of the highlights covered in the other itineraries. It includes Samburu National Reserve, Maralal, Loyangalani, Baringo, Bogoria and Nakuru.

—A less dramatic way to get to Lake Turkana is to charter a plane from Nairobi's Wilson Airport. The journey takes about 2 hours. See Practical Information *for charter companies—*

This is the most exhilarating trip in Kenya but it requires a lot of planning ahead. Only attempt it in a fully equipped, four-wheel-drive vehicle with spare jerry-cans of fuel and water and emergency food supplies (see advice in *Practical Information*). If you break down en route it may be some time before another vehicle passes by to come to your aid. Be prepared for at least two long, hot days of rough driving. Having said all that, it's worth every bump and ache to see the sunset over the jade sea.

Follow Itinerary 9 to **Samburu** (stay the first night) and then Itinerary 15 to **Maralal** (stay the second night).

Fill up with fuel and check your oil, tyres and water in Maralal the evening before setting off for Turkana. If you have any doubts about your vehicle, don't go! Recharge your video battery and order a picnic lunch from Maralal Safari

Slow transport

Lodge. Ask for an early morning call so that you can leave by first light next day.

The dirt c77 road from Kisima continues north to **Turkana** via Poror, Moridjo, Marti, Baragoi, South Horr and finally Loyangalani on the lake shore. It's only 214km (133 miles) but the road drops dramatically over 1,000m (3,280ft) and gradually deteriorates from corrugated and potholed dirt to a boulder-strewn track until the last 50km (31 miles) are little more than a broken trail over chunks of black lava spewed out of the earth thousands of years ago. The first place to take a break is **Baragoi**, about 97km (60 miles) away. Buy a soda and barter over the price of engraved gourds (probably full of camel's milk) at one of the *dukas* (grocers) in town. From Baragoi to the oasis town of South Horr is another 41km (25 miles). The final leg, to Loyangalani, 76km (47 miles) away, is the longest and roughest of all. En route you'll pass sporadic herds of cattle and Turkana, Samburu and Rendille people with their distinctive hairstyles and dress.

In **Loyangalani**, stay two nights at **Oasis Lodge** (Tel: 02-225255; PO Box 56707, Nairobi). By the time you arrive, all you'll want to do is jump in the pool and relax. If the weather is good, ask about visiting **South Island National Park**, 13km (8 miles) across the lake. This is not always possible as the wind which blows off Mount Kulal whips up sudden storms that easily capsize small craft. There's little there but volcanic ash and a few feral goats – in fact, it's probably the most barren place you'll ever visit, although crocodiles lay eggs on the island.

Next day, explore Loyangalani town's few *duka*. Ask one of the shopkeepers to fix up a guide who can take you to visit

El-Molo, Kenya's smallest tribe

the El-Molo people, the smallest tribe in Kenya who live a few kilometres further north, later in the day. Afterwards walk out to the lake shore past the huts of the Rendille people and bathe in the lake (take local advice on crocodile-free places).

In the afternoon, collect your guide (arrange his fee in advance – 200 shillings is usually acceptable) and visit the El-Molo people. For a few shillings or packets of biscuits you can take their photographs but it's polite to ask their permission first. Try to peep inside one of their igloo huts and go down to the water's edge to see their makeshift craft.

On the fifth day drive back to Maralal, and on the sixth day drive west to **Baringo** (see Itinerary 15). Return to Nairobi on the seventh day, stopping at **Bogoria** and **Nakuru** en route (Itinerary 10).

MOMBASA & THE COAST

*H*araka Haraka Haina Baraka – an old Swahili proverb meaning 'Put off today what you can do tomorrow' – sums up the pace of life on Kenya's coast.

The coastline stretches from Vanga, on the Tanzanian border in the south, to Malindi and Lamu in the north. Most of it is enclosed by a coral reef comprising four protected marine parks and home to more than 200 species of tropical fish. The reef is broken in only a few places – the deepest creeks are around Mombasa Island – so shark, marlin and other big game fish rarely swim close to the beach. The water is always warm – around 27–35ºC (80–95ºF) – while the shade temperature is about 35ºC (95ºF) and tempered by the cooling monsoon breezes that blow year-round. If a tropical beach paradise is what you're after, Kenya's coast is hard to beat.

Most of the itineraries in this section are based on Mombasa, a town whose eclectic history (see

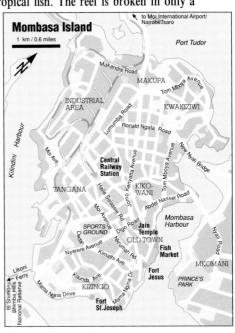

Dhow sailing

Mombasa

History and Culture) has left its mark in the old colonial British Club, tucked in the Arab old town among narrow streets overhung with *mashrabia* (enclosed balconies), and the pentagonal Fort Jesus, built by the Portuguese but now a favourite film-set of Hollywood directors (witness *Beau Geste*) and a popular spot for tying the knot – around 80 couples a year marry here. It is Kenya's second largest urbanisation and serves as a port for several east and central African countries. Originally centring on the 14 sq-km (5½ sq-mile) island, the city has now spilled on to the mainland, which has rapidly developed as a centre for package tourism.

Mombasa's old town is interesting to visit for its Islamic architecture and people, but don't plan to spend more than one day here. For all its history, there's little to do apart from shop or pray and the main points of interest can be covered in half a day. To get the most out of the city, hire the services of a local guide. Contact Universal Safari Tours Ltd (Tel: 011-316576/314541-3; PO Box 90030 Mombasa; Fax: 011-314544; Telex: 212338 UST KE). You will be taken to both the old and new town, and be shown the Indian temple, Fort Jesus and the main shopping areas.

After that, jump in your jeep, leave the city behind and explore (all my itineraries out of Mombasa start from the Elephant Tusks on Moi Avenue, close to the Castle Hotel). If you would prefer a more restful and, to my mind, nicer base than Mombasa, take off to Watamu and Malindi (see Itineraries 22 and 23), which can be reached by plane direct from Nairobi or by vehicle from Mombasa.

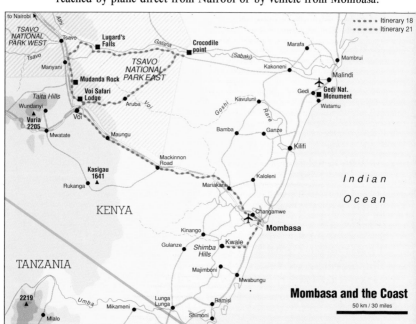

Mombasa and the Coast

50 km / 30 miles

Itinerary 18
Itinerary 21

Man-eaters in the making

17. Crocodiles and Crafts

An afternoon excursion from Mombasa to Mamba Crocodile Village, Bamburi Nature Park and Bombolulu Handicrafts Centre, followed by a night cruise and dinner on the *Tamarind* dhow.

−Telephone a few days in advance to reserve your table on the Tamarind *(011-20990/315569). Ask to be collected and returned to your hotel so that you don't have to drive at night. Dress on the dhow is casual but smart−*

Drive out of town along Moi Avenue towards Mombasa Harbour and turn left on to Digo Road which soon becomes Abdel Nasser Road. Turn left on to Tom Mboya Avenue and then right on to the B8 road to cross the harbour on the New Nyali Bridge. Your first destination is the **Mamba Crocodile Village** (Tel: 011-472709; open daily 8am–6pm) which is close to Nyali Beach opposite Nyali Golf Club. Turn right off the B8 on to the E982 and then follow the signposts. Plan to spend at least an hour here – there are hundreds of crocodiles of all sizes and ages to watch as well as horse-riding, camel-riding, botanical gardens and a restaurant serving crocodile meat.

From Mamba, drive along the E982 north up the coast to the junction with the main road (B8) from the New Nyali Bridge. Continue to drive north, towards Malindi, and shortly after the junction, on the left, you'll see the entrance to **Bamburi Quarry Nature Trail** (Tel: Mombasa 485729; open 2–5.30pm). This is an excellent example of land reclamation – in this case, what was once Africa's largest cement quarry has been transformed into a timber plantation and nature park, complete with buffalo, warthog, eland, oryx, monkeys and numerous birds as well as a fish farm, reptile pit and plant nursery with lots of indigenous tree species. Not quite so environmentally sound is the bottle-fed hippopotamus. Take a walk through the nature park.

On leaving Bamburi, drive back towards Mombasa, stopping off

Fort Jesus

at the **Bombolulu Handi-crafts Workshop** (Monday to Saturday 8am–6pm. Tel: 011-471704/473571/473572; PO Box 83988, Mombasa; Fax: 011-473570) off the B8 – follow the bright yellow signs. This workshop was set up to help hand-icapped Kenyans – who would otherwise be begging on the streets of Mombasa – find employment making traditional jewellery, wood carvings and leather-work for tourists to buy. It is a good place to watch skilled artisans at work and you know your money will be going directly to the craftsman (or woman).

Allow enough time to return to your hotel, change for dinner and pick up your transport to take you to the *Tamarind*.

The dhow leaves at 6.30pm on the dot. You can watch the sun set as you sip your cocktail and cruise past old Mombasa town and Fort Jesus and into Tudor Creek. The dhow will moor here while you eat – and you'd better be hungry. It serves the best seafood – including lobster and crab – you're likely to get anywhere on the coast, though there's steak too for non-fish eaters.

Afterwards you can dance to the music of the on-board band or just sit back and savour the night air. It's all a bit touristy, but no less enjoyable for all that. The dhow returns to the jetty at 10.30pm and you will be dropped off at your hotel or at a night-club (if you've still the energy) of your choice.

18. Hills, Forests and Waterfalls

Overnight excursion from Mombasa to Shimba Hills National Park, to see leopard baiting, elephants, rare sable antelope and Sheldrick Waterfalls. Take a sweater for the early morning.

This trip makes a cool change after the humidity of the coastal strip. Before setting out you should reserve your accommodation at Shimba Hills Lodge (Tel: Nyali Beach Hotel, Mombasa 011-471551, 471567/8; PO Box 83, Kwale) in advance. You'll need a four-wheel-drive vehicle.

Set off mid-morning and drive south out of Mombasa on the A14. Cross Kilindini Harbour with the Likoni car ferry (buy a few bags of cashew nuts and some sodas on the jetty for sustenance on your game drives) and continue driving south through the village of Waa. Shortly afterwards, on the right, turn off on to the C106 leading to Kwale.

The entrance to the **Shimba Hills National Reserve** is 3km (2 miles) after Kwale, along a good dirt road, and is well signposted.

The resident 'hunter' will meet you at the park gates and accompany you on a game drive through the hilly (rising up to 450m/1,476ft) coastal rain forest and back to the wooden lodge set in the old forest. En route, look out for the rare roan and sable antelope with their distinctive long, curved horns – this is the only place in Kenya you will see them. You'll also see old favourites (if you've followed other itineraries in this book) such as buffalo, hyena, water and reedbuck, giraffe, baboon and maybe even lion.

Shimba Hills National Reserve is one of the few game parks with an area set aside for walking, so make the most of the opportunity. After lunch at the lodge, walk down to **Sheldrick Waterfalls**, and be sure to make plenty of noise along the way to scare off any animals that might be thinking of drinking at the pool at the foot of the falls. To reach the falls, drive first to the **Elephant Lookout** (from here you can check to see if anything is lurking in the forest!). Walk down to the bottom of the valley and then follow the footpath through the trees, over the bridge and down to the falls.

After tea at the lodge, take another game drive before sundown and follow that with cocktails in the treehouse bar above the baited water-hole (all the bedrooms also face this), where you'll see lots of water birds and probably elephant and perhaps a leopard or two. The water-hole is floodlit at night – the animals seem to have got used to the idea of being permanently on stage, as they have in so many other parts of Kenya. There's also a beautiful view down to Diani Beach.

Next morning take an early game drive and see sunrise over the Indian Ocean. Return to the lodge for breakfast before setting off back for Mombasa.

Look for the elephants

19. Kisite-Mpunguti Coral Reef

A full-day excursion from Mombasa by motorised dhow to Shimoni and Kisite-Mpunguti Marine Reserve, which offers the best snorkelling in Kenya. Enjoy a five-course seafood lunch on Wasini Island followed by a visit to a Muslim village and coral gardens. Take sun-block, sun-hat, canvas shoes and bread (to feed the fish).

—For reservations, contact Wasini Island Restaurant and Kisite Marine Park Dhow Tours; Tel: 0127-2331 (direct) or 0127-2021/2/3; PO Box 281, Ukunda; Fax: 0127-3154—

If you don't want to drive, ask to be collected from your hotel when you make your reservation. If you drive, take the A14 out of Mombasa towards the Tanzanian border. Cross on to the mainland via the Likoni car ferry, then head south – there's only one road so you can't get lost. On the way you pass

On the way

through several small villages belonging to the Digo tribe, including Waa, Tiwi, Diani, Ukunda, Msambweni and Ramisi, as well as cashew, coconut and sugar plantations. About 3km (2 miles) past Ramisi turn left on to the D543 to **Shimoni**. In Kiswahili, Shimoni means 'Place of the Hole' and is named after the 15km-long (9-mile) cave where slaves were imprisoned before being shipped out. Shimoni is 75km (46 miles) from Mombasa.

The dhow leaves Shimoni jetty at 9am. You can hire snorkelling equipment here. To make sure your snorkel mask fits properly, hold it against your face without the strap, breathe in and look down at your feet. If the mask stays in place it will not leak in the water; if it falls off you need to try another one.

It's a 30-minute cruise between islets and along the reef to get to **Kisite-Mpunguti Marine Reserve**. Look out for dolphins on the way. The limpid waters here are the clearest along the coast which makes for ideal snorkelling conditions. Spend the morning swimming among the numerous species of coral fish – they'll swim closer if you

Handle with care

bring bread to feed to them – or relaxing on the dhow. Use plenty of sun-block and wear a T-shirt to protect yourself from the sun which burns twice as fiercely when it is reflected off water.

The morning's exercise will whet your appetite for the five-course seafood lunch on **Wasini Island**. Just 5km (3 miles) long and 1km

(½ mile) wide, Wasini used to be used as a shooting range during World War I and you can still find bits of scrap metal along the shoreline. Remember it's illegal and environmentally unfriendly to take the shells off the beach.

After lunch, either enjoy a siesta or visit the **Muslim village** and take a guided tour through the **coral gardens** behind (women should cover up to avoid offending the locals).

20. Lamu Island

A day trip by plane to Lamu Island, visiting a museum and a donkey sanctuary and taking a dhow trip through mangrove swamps. A barbecued seafood lunch, an old Arabic town.

–The best time to be in Lamu is during the week-long Maulidi (Prophet's birthday) celebrations (variable date). Muslims from all over East Africa flock to take part in the religious festivals, dancing, sword fights and feasts. Be sure to reserve your accommodation in advance (see Practical Information)–

You'll either love or hate Lamu, the oldest town in Kenya, but you should definitely pay it a visit. Once a powerful, independent, Swahili city state, this island situated 222km (138 miles) north of Malindi used to be so far off the beaten track that life there remained unchanged for centuries. Then in the 1970s the hippies arrived and Lamu has never looked back. Today the two cultures survive in uneasy symbiosis, paradoxically supported by the tourism that threatens both lifestyles.

But despite the *bangi* (marijuana) chewing dudes who pester every foreigner who walks the harbour front, Lamu still exudes a tranquil charm. The only car on the island belongs to the District

Basket-weaving in the mosque

Officer – everyone else uses donkeys, dhows and their own two feet to get about. The most obvious aspect of the island's Muslim culture (apart from the numerous mosques) is the absence of alcohol – only one or two hotels sell it. And the most common form of dress is a long white *kanzu* (gown) for men and the black *bui-bui* (ankle length cloak) for women.

To get there, take the morning flight from Malindi Airport to **Manda Island**. There are several airlines and they all operate similar schedules (see *Practical Information*). From Manda take the ferry across to **Lamu town**. Walk along the jetty, turn right and stroll along the harbour front for about 250m (800ft), past the Tourist Information Bureau and Standard Chartered Bank until you reach the **Lamu Museum** (open daily 8am–6pm). This is an excellent introduction to Swahili culture, and it is one of the best museums in Kenya; exhibits on display include a reconstruction of a Swahili house, dhows and intricately carved ivory *siwa* (traditional ceremonial musical instruments).

Come out of the museum and continue to walk along the harbour front. A few blocks further on you'll come to the **Donkey Sanctuary** where decrepit, sick or old donkeys enjoy a comfortable retirement. Walk 200m (650ft) beyond the donkeys to watch the woodcarvers at work making the intricately carved doors and lintels for which Lamu is famous.

Retrace your steps towards the jetty. On the way, haggle with the locals for a dhow to sail you to **Shela Beach** on the southernmost tip of the island, and back. In 1993 the going rate was less than a dollar a person. Ask to see the mangrove swamps on the way (though whether you can depends on the wind speed and direction). Stop off at Peponi's Hotel for an ice-cold beer and other drinks (Peponi's has a liquor licence) and have lunch in **Peponi's Barbecue Grill**, where the seafood is excellent.

Spend an hour or so on the beach and potter round the town. Eighteenth-century Arab houses tower over narrow streets, hiding inner courtyards where fountains play behind intricately carved screens.

Visit the market, where you will notice stalls selling betel nuts wrapped in leaves and wodges of *miraa* – both mild but addictive stimulants.

Lamu dhow

Lamu carved doors

Tourist shops have replaced many of the traditional craftshops but you can still find carved wood, silver jewellery and cowhorn *siwas*. Spend your last hour poking around, but don't be late for your flight. Small planes have to land back at Malindi before sundown and if your departure is delayed you will be stranded on Lamu until the following morning.

If you want to prolong your visit, buy the map/leaflet *Lamu: Map & Guide to the Archipelago, the Island and the Town* at the museum bookshop and stay at Peponi's (tel: 0121-3154; PO Box 24, Lamu; Telex: 21471) or The Island Hotel, both on Shela Beach (Tel: 0121-3290 or, in Nairobi, 02-229880; PO Box 179, Shela, Lamu).

You'll find plenty of things to do. Take a dhow trip to **Pate Island** 32km (20 miles) to the northeast of Lamu (talk to the dhow captains along the harbour front), visit the **Swahili House Museum**, a traditional house that has been lovingly restored, or take a boat to Matondoni village to see dhow-makers and basket-weavers.

21. Tsavo East National Park

Overnight trip to Tsavo East National Park, taking in elephants, crocodiles and plains game. See map on page 56.

From Mombasa, drive along Moi Avenue and turn left into Digo Road. Turn left again into Jomo Kenyatta Avenue, drive straight over the roundabout and continue over the Makupa causeway, towards Nairobi. Keep heading straight for 151km (94 miles) until you reach Voi. On the way look out for baobab trees which look as if they have been planted upside down with their roots in the air. If you come after the rains you may see them in flower.

Turn right at the signs towards the Voi Gate and **Voi Safari Lodge** (Tel: Voi 2121; Private Bag, Voi), where you are staying. Take the road to the left after the park entrance and drive up hill for 10km (6 miles) to get to the lodge. Look out for fringe-eared oryx on the way. Before lunch, take a swim in the pool and look for elephant at the watering-hole.

Voi Safari Lodge

The Tsavo East and West National

Poachers in Tsavo reduced the rhino population to 50

Parks comprise one of the largest game parks in the world, covering an area of 21,283 sq km (8,148 sq miles) or 4 percent of Kenya's land mass (you are in Tsavo East – Tsavo West is on the other side of the Nairobi-Mombasa road). There was mass poaching here in the early 1970s and 1980s which reduced the elephant population from around 55,000 to just 5,000 and the rhino population from 7,000 to fewer than 50. However, armed wardens and rangers trained by the British SAS (Special Air Service) and with a shoot-to-kill policy towards poachers have proved effective in curbing the slaughter and now numbers are on the increase again. There are more than 1,000 plant species and over 60 large mammal species. This park has well-graded roads that are linked together by numbered bollards at each junction so, despite its huge size, it is quite easy to navigate.

After lunch, game drive along the river or relax and bird-watch by the swimming-pool. After tea, climb to the top of the cliff behind the lodge for amazing views of the endless plains to the east and northeast.

Next morning drive 24km (15 miles) north past Irima and Magengani water-holes to **Mudanda Rock** (from bollards 165-147-158-166). It juts up above a dam where thousands of animals gather in the dry season. Drive back to bollard 158 and then head north for 50km (31 miles), past the **Buffalo Wallows** (bollard 169), to **Lugard's Falls** and **Crocodile Point** (bollards 160-161-162). Drive east to bollard 163, then turn south along **Rhino Ridge** to bollard 107 and bollard 138 for Aruba Dam and Lodge. Aruba Dam measures 85 hectares (210 acres) and is popular with elephant and plains game.

Turn right to get back to Voi, via the Kandera Swamp, and then retrace your route from here to Mombasa. Remember to leave enough time to get back to Mombasa before nightfall.

Alternatively, you can turn right at Voi to drive on to Nairobi, 333km (217 miles) away. To arrive in Nairobi before sunset allow at least 5 hours for the journey. It is a long and tiring drive.

22. Watamu

A morning drive to Watamu, where you will stay.

–Though Watamu, along with Malindi (see Itinerary 23), can be visited from Mombasa, it makes a very agreeable base, particularly for those who prefer a quieter scene than the one in Mombasa. This itinerary is therefore designed as a linear rather than circular tour, and assumes you will want to stay in Watamu for a few days. The drive takes about 2 hours–

From Mombasa, cross over Nyali Bridge back to the mainland and drive north up the B8. It's a beautiful drive, passing by baobab trees, palms, a sisal estate and numerous mosques. Kilifi Creek, 59km (37 miles) to the north, is now spanned by a bridge built by the Japanese and opened in 1992. If the queue isn't too long, turn off just before the bridge and take the car ferry across. Buy a bag of salted cashew nuts on the jetty to nibble on the way – it takes about 15 minutes and gives you a chance to chat with the locals.

On the other side, you're now 64km (40 miles) from Malindi. To get to Watamu, head north and turn right at the Gedi turn-off on to the E899. It is well sign-posted. This road will take you past the entrance to the Gedi Ruins (see Itinerary 23) and on to Watamu village.

Peace

Despite the influx of tourism **Watamu** has lost little of its sleepy, fishing village atmosphere. You can still see fishermen paddling ashore in their makeshift dhows and you won't be bombarded by the ubiquitous beach touts trying to sell you things that you don't really want. There's not much to do in the village itself (except hire bicycles and post letters) although it is interesting to contrast the simplicity of the local people's lifestyle and tumbledown *makuti* (palm-thatched) cottages with the opulence of the five tourist hotels lining the beach to the south.

The best hotel is Hemingways, named after Ernest Hemingway who used to come deep-sea fishing from this bay. In fact, this part of the Indian Ocean is still the haunt of craggy old fishermen recounting endless tales of 'the one they let go'. **Hemingways Deep Sea Fish-**

Into the water backwards

Sokoke-Scops owl

ing and **Watersports Centre** in the hotel lobby can arrange horse-riding (8.30–10.30am, 4–5pm and 5.30–6.30pm), tennis, golf (at Malindi Golf and Country Club), camel treks, bird-watching, waterskiing and a barbecue on Mida Creek. Alternatively contact Richard Bennet at **Turtle Bay Hotel** (Tel: 0122-32003/32080; PO Box 457, Malindi; Fax: 0122-32268; Telex 0987-21074 TURTLEB) to fix up a guided tour through the Arabuko-Sokoke forest, a few kilometres inland from Watamu. The forest covers more than 320 sq km (124 sq miles) and is home to various mammals, from elephants to elephant-shrews, as well as birds (including the Sokoke-Scops owl and hundreds of insects and butterflies). Richard, who is an Oxford University zoologist, knows the reserve intimately and can name all the wildlife you come across.

23. Malindi

A full-day excursion to Malindi from Watamu, taking in Gedi Ruins, a snake park and falconry centre, and rounding off the day at a beachclub.

–Providing you don't mind pedalling against the wind in one direction, this is a great bicycle trip (hire cycles from Watamu village)–

From Watamu, drive back for about 2½ km (1¾ miles) along the E899 towards Gedi. Turn off along a gravel road on the right just before the T-junction. The **Gedi Ruins** are a kilometre (half a mile) further along.

The crumbled remains of this Arab-Swahili town are built out of coral and are believed to date back to the 13th century. They were discovered in the 1920s and the site is still surrounded by Tarzanesque jungle, with lizards, monkeys and butterflies darting among the crumbling stones. There are the remains of a palace, several mosques, tombs and houses with painted plaster walls. Most surprising of all are the remnants of seemingly modern bathrooms with double washbasins and bidets.

Allow at least an hour to visit the site; you can buy an excellent guidebook and map at the entrance.

Afterwards return to the E899 and turn right to get to the T-junction. Turn right on to the B8 and drive towards Malindi town. Go past the turn-off for the airport and then straight ahead at the

Ruins of the Arab-Swahili town at Gedi

roundabout. Go straight ahead again at the crossroads. At the next crossroads (with the police station on the left and the post office on the right) turn left, driving parallel to the ocean. Keep driving past Barclays Bank and the shopping centre until you come to the Stardust Club on the left. Turn left at the next junction. The **snake park** and **falconry centre** are towards the end of this block on the left. Allow about an hour to visit each.

By now you'll be hot and sticky and in need of a swim and refreshments. I suggest you head for the **Driftwood Club** which is on the outskirts of town. To get there turn left out of the snake park and then left again at the crossroads. Keep driving as far as the T-junction which is signposted to Nairobi. Turn left, then right at the mosque (Uhuru Park is on the diagonally opposite corner). At the next T-junction turn left, then left again at the youth hostel. You will now be heading back towards the sea. At the T-junction turn right to drive along parallel with the coast until you come to the Driftwood Club. The small temporary membership fee entitles you to swim in the pool (or ocean) or just relax at the bar (great snacks and Bloody Marys).

To get back to Watamu, retrace your steps to the youth hostel previously mentioned in directions above. Turn right at the T-junction and continue until you reach the roundabout. Turn left. You're now back on the main B8 road to Gedi, Watamu or Mombasa.

Relax

Kenya is known for its game parks (see p17–18 for discussion of the parks' purposes and problems). The following are referred to in the Wildlife Checklist: Aberdare National Park, Amboseli National Park, Buffalo Springs National Reserve, Lake Bogoria National Reserve, Lake Nakuru National Park, Masai Mara National Reserve, Nairobi National Park, Samburu National Reserve, Shaba National Reserve, Tsavo East and Tsavo West National Parks. National Parks are controlled by the Kenya Wildlife Services, a government body. National Reserves are controlled by the local county councils.

The best times to spot game are at dawn and dusk when most animals feed, and the ideal time to take photographs is early morning or late afternoon. Detailed maps of the parks are readily available.

The Wildlife Checklist includes mammals, insects and reptiles, with a separate section on birds. It is not comprehensive, but is a good guide to what to look out for and where.

Get close to game without leaving your vehicle

Wildlife Checklist

Animal	*Where found*
African wild cat	Widely distributed.
Antelope: sable	Shimba Hills. Rare.
Antelope: roan	Masai Mara, Shimba Hills. Quite rare.
Baboon	Aberdares, Nairobi Park, Amboseli, Tsavo, Samburu.
Bat-eared fox	Amboseli, Nairobi Park, all areas very rare.
Bongo	Aberdares, Mount Kenya.
Buffalo	Tsavo, Samburu, Amboseli, Masai Mara. Widely distributed.
Bush pig	Rarely seen. Nocturnal. Forests and bushy savannah.
Bushbaby	Widely distributed, but nocturnal. Forests and bushlands.
Bushbuck	Nairobi Park. Dense bushlands.
Chameleon: horned	Widespread.
Cheetah	Nairobi Park, Amboseli, Samburu, Masai Mara. Grasslands.
Dik-dik	Tsavo, Amboseli, Masai Mara, Samburu. Dry bush country.
Duiker	Forests, dense bushlands, high grass. Rarely seen.
Dung beetle	Everywhere but especially Tsavo area at start of rains.
Eland	Nairobi Park, Tsavo, Masai Mara. Grasslands, mountain moorlands.
Elephant	Aberdares, Tsavo, Masai Mara, Mount Kenya, Amboseli, Samburu.
Gazelle: Thomson's	Nairobi Park, Amboseli, Masai Mara. Grasslands and savannah.
Gazelle: Grant's	Tsavo, Nairobi Park, Amboseli, Masai Mara, Samburu. Grasslands and savannah.
Genet (various)	Nocturnal. Often seen at camps and lodges.
Gerenuk	Tsavo, Samburu, Amboseli, Lake Magadi. Dry bush.
Giant forest hog	Aberdares, Mount Kenya. Forests.
Giant millipede	Tree trunks and fallen leaves. Undergrowth.
Giraffe: Masai	Tsavo, Nairobi Park, Masai Mara, Amboseli, southern Kenya.
Giraffe: Reticulated	Samburu, northern Kenya.
Giraffe: Rothschild's	Nakuru.
Hartebeest	Open grasslands.
Hippopotamus	Masai Mara, Tsavo, Amboseli. Rivers, swamps and lakes.
Honey badger	Nocturnal. Often seen near camps and lodges.
Hunting dog	Tsavo, Masai Mara, Samburu, Nairobi Park. Rare.
Hyrax: rock	Nairobi Park.
Hyrax: tree	Nocturnal. Forests.
Impala	Tsavo, Nairobi Park, Amboseli, Masai Mara, Samburu.
Jackal: black or silver-backed	Amboseli, Nairobi Park, Masai Mara. Grasslands.
Klipspringer	Bogoria, Naivasha.
Kudu: greater	Shimba Hills, Bogoria and Samburu. Rare.
Kudu: lesser	Tsavo, Amboseli, northern Kenya
Leopard	All parks. Secretive.
Lion	Nairobi Park, Masai Mara, Tsavo, Amboseli, Samburu. Grasslands, open bushlands, semi-desert.
Lizard: Nile monitor	Rivers.
Lizard: Agama	Lodges and camps (males blue with red heads).
Lizard: spotted monitor	Savannah and dry bush.
Mongoose (various)	Widely distributed.
Monkey: Sykes	Widely distributed.
Monkey: red colobus	Arabuko-Sokoke forest.
Monkey: vervet	Widely distributed.
Monkey: colobus	Mount Kenya, Aberdares, Nakuru. Highland forests.
Nile crocodile	Tsavo, Samburu, Shaba, Masai Mara, Nairobi Park. Rivers, lakes and swamps.
Oribi	Grasslands, open woodlands. Very rare.
Oryx: Beisa	Samburu, northern Kenya.

Oryx: fringe-eared	Tsavo, Amboseli.
Otter	Widely distributed – lakes, rivers, etc.
Reedbuck: Chanler's mountain	Nairobi Park. Rocky slopes and escarpments.
Reedbuck: Bohor	Nairobi Park, Nakuru. Grasslands with bushes.
Rhinoceros: black	Tsavo, Nairobi Park, Amboseli, Masai Mara, Mount Kenya, Aberdares, Nakuru.
Rhinoceros: white	Nakuru, Solio Ranch.
Scorpions	Hot, dry bush.
Serval cat	Widely distributed but rarely seen.
Snake: black mamba	Rare.
Snake: green tree	Slithering along tree branches.
Snake: puff adder	Widespread. Bush and scrub. Samburu.
Snake: rock python	Widely distributed but rarely seen.
Snake: spitting cobra	Widespread.
Spotted hyena	Widely distributed.
Steinbok	Grasslands.
Suni	Highland and coastal forests, dense bushlands.
Topi	Masai Mara.
Tortoise	Savannah and grasslands.
Turtle	Sea, streams and rivers.
Warthog	Savannah and bushy grasslands. Everywhere.
Waterbuck	Tsavo, Amboseli, Nairobi Park, Samburu.
Waterbuck: Defassa	Tsavo, Amboseli, Nairobi Park, Nakuru.
Wildebeest	Masai Mara, southern Kenya, Amboseli.
Zebra: Burchell's	Masai Mara, Amboseli. Open grasslands.
Zebra: Grevy's	Samburu, northern Kenya.

Bird Checklist

African spoonbill	Rift Valley lakes, lagoons and dams.
Barbet	Many species.
Barbet: red and yellow	Tsavo, Samburu. Dry termite mounds.
Barbet: D'Arnaud's	Interesting mating behaviour.
Bee-eater: carmine	Coastal areas.
Bee-eater: cinnamon-chested	Mount Kenya region.
Bee-eater: little	Widely distributed.
Bee-eater: white-fronted	Naivasha.
Black crake	Walking on hippo's back. Marshes, swamps, lakes and river shores.
Bustard: black-bellied	Masai Mara, Tsavo. Cultivated areas and open grasslands.
Bustard: kori	Nairobi Park, Amboseli, Samburu, Masai Mara. Open savannah and thorn bush.
Buzzard: augur	Mountains, savannah, cultivated areas.
Cormorant	Naivasha and Nakuru.
Courser	Dry bush country.
Crowned crane	Widely distributed.
Eagle: African fish	Along rivers, estuaries, etc.
Eagle: Bateleur	Open savannah and thornbush country.
Eagle: martial	Nairobi Park. Widely distributed.
Eagle: tawny	Widely distributed.
Eagle: Verreaux's	Nairobi Park. Rocky hills, mountains.
Egret: cattle	Widely distributed, often with grazing flocks.
Egret: yellow-billed	Swamps, rivers, lakes.
Falcon	Many species.
Finches	Widely distributed.
Flamingo: greater	Lakes Magadi and Nakuru.
Flamingo: lesser	Lakes Magadi, Bogoria and Nakuru.
Francolin	Widespread
Francolin: Jackson's	Aberdares, Mount Kenya. Mountain forests.
Geese: Egyptian	Widely distributed.

Geese: knob-billed	Lake Naivasha. Lakes, pools and wooded swamps.
Geese: spurwing	Lakes and rivers.
Goshawk: pale chanting	Acacia and bush country.
Guineafowl: helmeted	Widely distributed.
Guineafowl: vulturine	Samburu. Dry bush. Northern Kenya.
Gull	Inland waters and at coast.
Hadada	Nairobi Park, Naivasha.
Hawk	Several species.
Heron: night	Naivasha and Nakuru.
Heron: Goliath	Lake Naivasha. Never far from water.
Heron: black-headed	Common.
Honey guide	Indicate location of bee's nest.
Hoopoe	Woodland and riverine forest.
Hornbill	Widely distributed.
Hornbill: ground	Savannah. Forages on ground.
Ibis	Widely distributed.
Jacana	See Lily trotter.
Kingfisher	Many species. Usually near water.
Kite: yellow-billed	Savannah, lakes, rivers, towns.
Kite: black-shouldered	Nairobi Park. Grasslands and cultivated areas.
Lily trotter	Naivasha, Amboseli.
Mousebird	Forest edges, bushy savannah, scrub and cultivated areas.
Nightjar	Many species. Distinctive call.
Ostrich: Somali	Samburu, north-eastern Kenya.
Ostrich: Masai	Widely distributed in grasslands.
Owl: Verreaux's eagle	Acacia trees in riverine forest or savannah.
Owl: African marsh	High grass.
Oxpecker: red/yellow-billed	On animal's backs.
Parrot: red-headed	Mountain forests.
Pelican	Naivasha and Nakuru. Inland lakes.
Plover	Many species. Rift Valley lakes, Samburu, Lake Magadi. Swamps, mudflats, grasslands, lakes, rivers, dams, etc.
Purple gallinule	Naivasha. Swamps and papyrus marshes.
Red-crested coot	Naivasha. Lakes, dams and swamps.
Roller: broad-billed	Forests, savannah, riverine forests and mountain areas up to bamboo.
Roller: lilac-breasted	Savannah and dry bush.
Sand grouse	Several species, widely distributed.
Secretary bird	Grasslands and light bush country.
Shrike: fiscal	Ubiquitous.
Starling: superb	Lodges and picnic sites. Common.
Starling: golden-breasted	Tsavo.
Stone curlew	Three species: one in dry scrub and open woodlands, two near water.
Stork: marabou	Widely distributed.
Stork: hammerkop	Rivers, pools, shallow lake shores.
Stork: saddle-billed	Amboseli, Masai Mara, Buffalo Springs. Swamps, marshes and reedy lake shores.
Stork: Abdim's	Comes in from Sudan in large flocks.
Stork: yellow-billed	Widely distributed near water.
Stork: open-billed	Lakes, marshes and large lagoons.
Sunbirds	Many species.
Toko	See hornbill.
Trogon: Narina's	Highland and mountain forest.
Turaco	Coastal highland and mountain forest.
Turaco: grey	Savannah and dry bush.
Vultures	Many species and widely distributed, particularly near kills.
Weavers	Many species.
White-bellied go-away bird	Samburu.
Woodpecker	Many species.
Wydah birds	Many species.

Eating Out

Kenyans breakfast on *mandazi* (a triangular-shaped doughnut) washed down with sweet milky tea. Lunch is *ugali* (corn meal porridge) eaten with vegetable or meat stew. Dinner might be *nyama choma* (grilled meat, often goat) and *sukuma wiki* (spinach). Other dishes include *irio* (soaked green peas cooked with potatoes and maize) and *githeri* (red beans and maize with potatoes, carrots, spinach, tomatoes and onions). They're all worth trying but will not necessarily please palates used to more piquant flavours.

Though the national cuisine is somewhat bland, the wide and delicious range of other foods on offer more than makes up for it. Fish-eaters can indulge in lobster, prawns, crayfish, Nile perch, tilapia (a fresh water fish similar to perch), parrot fish, or delicious smoked sailfish, the Kenyan equivalent to smoked salmon. Meat-eaters can eat their fill of zebra, gazelle, crocodile, giraffe, ostrich, or the rather more ordinary beef or Molo lamb. Healthy eating enthusiasts can tuck into passion fruit, paw-paw, guavas, pineapple, plums, oranges, bananas and other fruits. To see and sample the wide range of fresh produce on offer, you should call into Nairobi's City Market (see *Shopping*).

No-one should miss warm toasted cashew, macadamia and coconuts, or avocados with Worcestershire sauce. Or plantain, arrowroot or cassava chips. And so the list goes on.

On the drinking front, the four great Kenyan beers are Pilsner Tusker and White Cap (in large bottles), Tusker Premium (the most expensive and strongest) and Tusker Export (the small bottle).

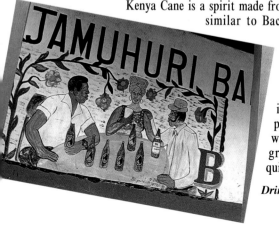

Kenya Cane is a spirit made from sugar cane and tastes similar to Bacardi. Kenya Gold is a coffee liqueur.

There are two sorts of wine: Papaya wine, which tastes a bit like very bad home-brew and is best avoided if at all possible; and Naivasha white wine, made from grapes, which is usually quite palatable.

Drinking locally

Restaurants

Eating out is one of the great pleasures of Kenya. There are plenty of excellent restaurants in Nairobi and, even at the most expensive, you'd be hard pressed to spend much more than 1,000 shillings ($13–15) per person excluding wine.

Nairobi

THE KENTMERE CLUB
On the old Limuru Road
Tel: 0154-42053/42101
My favourite restaurant, set in an old staging house and with beautiful gardens. Try mushrooms in a white wine and Camembert sauce followed by grilled *tilapia*. If you eat out only once, make sure it's here.

The Carnivore (see below)

CARNIVORE
Off Langata Road
Tel: 02-501775
Open daily noon–2.30pm and 7–10.30pm. If you ever wanted to know what zebra, giraffe, ostrich, crocodile, impala and other wild meats taste like, this is the place for you. Great haunches of meat are spit-roasted on swords and then carved directly on to your plate. Eat as much as you like. (There's also an *à la carte* and vegetarian menu for those with alternative appetites). You should try a *dawa* (vodka, honey and lime juice) before you start.

TAMARIND
National Bank House, Harambee Avenue
Tel: 02-338959
Open: Monday to Saturday noon–2.30pm and daily 7pm–12.30am. The best seafood away from the coast. Try the Prawns Piri Piri or any of the crab dishes.

French/International

HORSEMAN
Ngong Road/Langata Road, Karen
Tel: 02-882782
Open daily 7–11.30pm. One of the best restaurants in Nairobi, set in an old colonial house. Intimate atmosphere. Try their Zanzibari fish and coconut soup. Excellent pepper steak.

IBIS GRILL
Norfolk Hotel, Harry Thuku Road
Tel: 02-335422
Open daily 12.30–2pm and 7.30–10pm. The French *nouvelle cuisine* is exquisite. Beautiful surroundings and good service.

Italian

LA GALLERIA
Westlands Road (in the international casino complex)
Tel: 02-742600/744477
Open Monday to Friday 12.30–2.30pm, Monday to Saturday 7.30–10.30pm. The best Italian restaurant in town. Try *carpaccio* (thinly sliced raw beef, sprinkled with olive oil and Parmesan cheese and eaten with warm bread and butter) or the mixed seafood platter. You can buy the original paintings decorating the walls. Free entry to the casino is included in the price of a meal.

TOONA TREE
Westlands Road (in the international casino complex)
Tel: 02-744477
Open 12.30–2pm (3pm on Saturday

Good place for a sundowner

and Sunday) and 7–11pm. Named after the enormous toona tree shading the outdoor tables, this restaurant is a great place for lunch. Try their seafood pizza or *gnocchi* with pesto. They also have an extensive salad bar. Live music on Friday nights. Free entry to the casino for all clients.

Japanese

AKASAKA
Standard Street
Tel: 02-220299
Open daily 12.30–2pm and 6.30–11pm. The best Japanese in town. Try a lunch box – soup, chicken, sushi, tempura fish or meat with rice, stir-fried vegetables and salad and green tea.

Indian

NAWAB TANDOORI
Muthaiga Shopping Centre, Limuru Road. Tel: 02-740209/740292
Open daily noon–3pm and 7–10.30pm. Specialists in North Indian and Tandoori cuisine. The prawn *masala*, *palak aloo* (creamed spinach with potatoes) and *dal nawabi* (lentils) are particularly good.

Chinese

THE CHINA PLATE
Accra/Taveta Road, off Tom Mboya Street. Tel: 02-225225

Open daily noon–2.30pm and 7–10.30pm. Specialists in spicy Szechuan dishes. Ginger crab and braised prawns Szechuan-style are especially good.

For Breakfast

SAFARI PARK HOTEL
Thika Road
Tel: 02-802493
Open daily 7.30–10am

Mombasa and the Coast

Generally speaking, the food in the coast hotels is excellent and most people tend to eat in their hotel and then take advantage of the in-house entertainment.

Watamu is only a tiny village and has only one supermarket, let alone any restaurants. I suggest you try the restaurants in various hotels listed. **Hemingways** has an excellent seafood buffet lunch on Sunday and their restaurant is worth visiting any day of the week.

In Mombasa town, the **Manor Hotel**, Nyerere Avenue, PO Box 84851, Mombasa (Tel: Mombasa 011-314634) serves excellent food for lunch; and the **Nyali Beach Hotel** has five different restaurants (Italian, Asian/Arab, African, Seafood and Oriental).

Shopping

Baskets and Textiles

The ubiquitous woven sisal baskets known as *kiondos* are every-where. They're very useful, and thief-proof for carrying valuables around. Also common are Kisii stone carvings, soap dishes and bowls (either in its natural pink and white form or, the latest fash-ion, brightly painted and engraved) and wood carvings depicting Kenyan animals and tribespeople; look out for the Giacometti-like figures carved out of a single branch. Brightly-coloured textiles in-clude *batiks* on silk or cotton and cotton *kangas/kikois*, tradition-ally worn as wrap-arounds for men and women, but great for cush-ion covers too.

Hand-woven cloth and rugs in cotton or wool are coloured with natural or synthetic dyes. Buy tablecloths, napkins, bedspreads or simply reams of fabric to cover furniture, make cushions, etc.

Less traditional but very characteristic are T-shirts. Look for the colourful designs of Hardcore, Tinga Tinga or Dash.

Jewellery and Glass

Traditional and modern designs incorporate silver, amber, shells, coral, copper wire, leather, feathers, etc. Semi-precious stones (red and green garnet, malachite, tiger eye etc) are also used. On the coast, look for Arab designs in silver. For glassware, look out for hand-blown goblets and other tableware reminiscent of medieval drinking vessels in thick blue or green glass full of air bubbles.

Woodwork

Intricately carved out of *mvuli* wood with brass or silver bindings, studs and locks, Zanzibari chests come in various sizes. You will also find desks and coffee tables in similar designs.

Equally handsome are Lamu beds. These look won-derful with lots of *kikoi*- and *kanga*-covered cushions. You can buy just the carved legs in Kenya then have the finished article assembled back home.

Hand-made wooden picture frames and trays are attrac-tive, some inlaid with brass.

Basket weaving

All sorts of traditional items

Where to Shop

Nairobi

CITY MARKET
Between Muindi Mbingu and Koinange Streets
Open Monday to Friday 7.30am–6pm, Saturday 7.30am–4pm, Sunday 8am–1pm. For fruit, vegetables, crafts, baskets, Kisii stone-carvings, batiks, etc.

AFRICAN HERITAGE
Kenyatta Avenue
Open Monday to Saturday 9.30am–6pm and Sunday 11am–4pm and *Libra House, Mombasa Road*
Open Monday to Friday 9.30am–6pm, Saturday 9.30am–10pm, Sunday 11am–4pm. Both branches boast an extensive collection of beautifully made arts and crafts from all over Africa, including furniture, masks, carvings, paintings and batiks, baskets, jewellery and religious icons. It's not the cheapest place but the quality is superb – come here before going to other craft markets so that you can compare what's on offer. Their new Libra House shop on the road out to the airport is mind-boggling (you'll probably spend more than you planned). Go on a Sunday to watch their floorshow.

KICHAKA
Kijabe Street
Open Monday to Friday 9.30am–1pm and 2–5.30pm and Saturday 9am–1pm. This shop has the best collection of Kenyan-made crafts in Nairobi, including rugs, picture frames, hand-blown glass, tablecloths and napkins, clothing, mirrors, Kisii stone, trays, crockery, etc. The shop also has wonderful clothing made of hand-dyed cotton.

UNDUGU SHOP
Woodvale Grove, Westlands (around the corner from the market)
Open Monday to Friday 9am–5.30pm and Saturday 9am–5pm. *Undugu* means 'brotherhood' in Kiswahili and this shop was founded to help unemployed youths. The locally made arts and crafts, similar to those at Spinner's Web and Kichaka, are excellent quality and much cheaper than elsewhere. Profits go towards community homes for street children, preventive health care, training, etc.

THE CRAFT MARKET and OUT OF TOWN
ABC Place, Waiyaki Way
Open Monday to Saturday 9am–6pm and Sunday 9am–1pm. Great selection of knitwear, jewellery, baskets and other crafts.

Mombasa shop

THE GLASS GALLERY
Lonrho House, Kaunda Street
Open Monday to Saturday 9am–6pm.
The most elegant shop in Nairobi.
Resident artist Pippa Simpson en-
graves African images on glass goblets, vases, perfume bottles, mirrors,
bowls, etc. Discuss your design with
her personally. There is also a range
of stained glassware on offer, including window panels and lampshades,
and antique silver jewellery. All pur-
chases can be shipped.

KASHMIR CRAFTS
Biashara Street (near Moktar Daddar Street)
Open Monday to Friday 8.30am–
12.30pm and 2–5.30pm, Saturday
8.30am–12.30pm and 1.30–4.30pm.
If you can't find what you want, talk
to Ramesh – he can unearth just
about anything and his prices are
very competitive. Ask to see his carved
Zanzibari chests, made by his cousin
in Mombasa, and his amber and silver beads. He has a wonderful collection of jewellery and can make up
earrings, necklaces, rings and
brooches at very reasonable prices.

UTMADUNI (Crafts for Conservation)
*Bogani East Road off Langata Road
(near the Giraffe Sanctuary), Karen*
Open Monday to Sunday 9.30am–6pm.
This enormous house has different
boutiques in each room, including a
children's toy shop and play area, an
art and crafts outlet, a tea room and
an art gallery. Good for lunch.

SIAFU
Next to the Horseman Restaurant, Karen
Open Monday to Saturday 9.30am–
1pm and 2–5.30pm. Sells unusual
gifts, including crudely carved and
brightly painted wooden birds, jig-
saw puzzles, rocking giraffes, zebra
swings and elephant book ends.

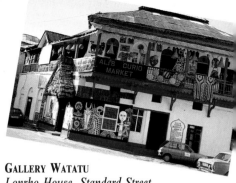

GALLERY WATATU
Lonrho House, Standard Street
Open daily 9.30am–6pm. A diverse
collection of Kenyan art includes
sculptures and paintings by internationally recognised artists, such as
Jak Katarikawe and Sane Wadu, as
well as talented newcomers. Talk to
the sales assistants; they have a genuine love for African art and are
knowledgeable about the artists.
Prices start at around 1,500 shillings.

SARANG ART GALLERY
Standard Street
Open Monday to Saturday 9am–
5.30pm. Similar to Gallery Watatu
but not as expensive. Good collection
of wood and stone sculptures.

Mombasa
It is best to shop in Nairobi but,
failing that, browse along Biashara
Street and call in and look at any
shop that takes your fancy. There
are also lots of handicraft stalls,
with wood and soap stone carvings,
hats, beads, bangles, and *kiondos*
near the hotels. In particular, the
shops near the Serena Beach Hotel
(come out of the hotel, turn right
and walk 100m/330ft along the
road) and some wonderful old
wooden statues, headdresses, stools
and tables from all over Africa.
Unfortunately prices are very
inflated. Specific recommendations
for Mombasa shops include AFRICAN
HERITAGE which has a shop in the
Serena Beach Hotel, and BOMBULU
HANDICRAFTS VILLAGE.

Practical Information

GETTING THERE

By Air

There are two international airports: the recently renovated (1993) Jomo Kenyatta Airport in Nairobi, 16km (10 miles) from the city centre, and Moi International Airport in Mombasa. Both airports are connected by domestic flights.

By Sea and Train

Regular passenger sevices to Mombasa were suspended in the 1970s. Few cargo ships offer passenger berths and cruise liners only make occasional calls.

No direct access is possible by rail.

By Road

Road transit through northeast and northwest Africa is uncertain. Overland safari companies still do it and fly over difficult areas – but the journey is long and hard.

You can travel by road from Somalia, Ethiopia, Tanzania or Uganda but the

Kilimanjaro

roads can be dangerous, especially at night. If you have only a short time in East Africa it's probably better to fly in.

TRAVEL ESSENTIALS

When to Visit

To see the wildebeest migration in the Masai Mara, come in July/August. But Kenya is beautiful at any time of year.

Visas, Passports and Documents

All visitors must have a valid passport. A visa is required by everyone except British Commmonwealth citizens. You can apply for one from any Kenyan Embassy, Consulate or High Commission or from a British Embassy in countries where Kenya has no diplomatic representation. You can also get one at the airport, but expect long queues.

If you intend to hire a vehicle while in Kenya, bring your domestic or international driving licence.

Vaccinations and Health Precautions

There have been cases of yellow fever in Kenya so it's best to get vaccinated at least 10 days before travelling. However, a yellow fever vaccination certificate is only mandatory if you arrive from endemic areas. It's also highly advisable to take precautions against typhoid, hepatitus A, tetanus and polio.

Malaria is endemic below altitudes of

1,830m (6,000ft). Begin taking a course of prophylactics (Paludrin and Chloroquine are the best) two weeks before travelling, and continue taking them throughout your stay and for two weeks after your return home. Better still, avoid getting bitten. Mosquitoes bite mainly at dusk and during the night and you're particularly at risk in game parks and on the coast. Use insect repellant liberally and wear long sleeves, trousers and socks after sundown. Sleep under a mosquito net or in an air-conditioned room if possible. If you develop influenza-like symptoms within six weeks of arriving home, you should insist on being tested for malaria, preferably at your nearest tropical diseases hospital.

Customs

Visitors can bring in 200 cigarettes or 50 cigars, 1 litre of alcohol and ¼ of a litre of perfume, duty free. You may have to pay a refundable deposit on videos, tape recorders, etc, at the port of entry.

Climate

The equatorial sun is deceptively intense and protective sun-cream and a hat are essential. Heat stroke combined with the high altitude can be particularly unpleasant so avoid rushing around in the midday sun.

There are two rainy seasons: the long rains from the end of March to early June and the short rains from mid-October to mid-December. Much of the rain falls from late afternoon through the night, often with hot and sunny mornings.

The dry season is from early January to the end of March. The cool dry season is mid-June to early October.

Coastal areas remain hot all year round, tempered by monsoon breezes. Higher land areas can be warm during the day but quite cool at night.

Clothing

Bring loose-fitting cotton clothes with a light woollen sweater or jacket for warmth in the evenings. Comfortable walking shoes are essential.

Dress in Kenya is casual, but scant or provocative clothing may cause offence so use your common sense and tact, particularly in areas with a high Muslim population. Topless sunbathing and nudity are not allowed anywhere.

Electricity

The standard supply is 240 volts (50 cycles AC). Bring a small step-down voltage converter if you want to use 110 volt appliances.

Time Zones

Kenya is three hours ahead of Greenwich Mean Time.

GETTING ACQUAINTED

Geography

Straddling the equator, Kenya's 582,644 sq km (224,960 sq miles) include almost every type of geographic landform, from a snow-capped mountain to true desert.

Where next?

Bound on three sides by Ethiopia, Sudan, Somalia, Uganda and Tanzania, her 483km (300 miles) of tropical coastline fringe the Indian Ocean, with a coral reef running the length of the coast that is a marine Eden – much of it protected as marine national parks.

Kenya's capital Nairobi ('the city in the sun') is in the south of the country at an altitude of 1,670m (5,479ft). The population of Nairobi is about 1.6 million.

Government and Economy

Kenya's first multi-party elections since independence were held in December 1992. The incumbent president, Daniel arap Moi, was re-elected, to the dismay of many Kenyans who believe he rigged the voting. However, Moi's party, the Kenya African National Union (KANU), is no longer the only party in Parliament and Kenyan politics are likely to be stormy in the future.

Part of Kenya's recent social unrest stems from the hardship caused by the 1993 devaluation of the Kenyan shilling. Unfortunately such devaluations are unlikely to benefit the tourist in the short or long term; as most big prices are now quoted in hard currency such as US dollars, and converted on the day.

Kenya is still one of the most prosperous countries in black Africa. Tourism is the greatest source of foreign revenue, surpassing tea, coffee and horticultural exports collectively (the next biggest earners) combined.

Religion

About 70 percent of Kenyans are Christian (Anglican, Baptist, Coptic, Catholic, Orthodox, Pentecostal and Presbyterian) with numerous Afro-Christian sects. About 20 percent of the population are Islamic and approximately 10 percent are Sikhs and Hindus.

Islam is strong on the coast

How Not to Offend

Kenyans are very polite, friendly and hospitable. Greetings are important and no conversation begins without first saying *Jambo* (Kiswahili for 'hello') or *Habari gani?*('how are things?') Unknown men should be addressed as *Bwana*, or *Mzee* for older men. Women should be addressed as *Mama*.

Petting in public is frowned upon. Men often hold hands in friendship but you rarely see anyone behaving more intimately in public. Nude or topless bathing is not allowed.

Population Mix

There are more than 40 different ethnic groups in Kenya, many with their own languages, but English is the official language and Kiswahili the national language. In urban areas most people speak English or Kiswahili and their own tribal language.

Kenya's population is estimated to be 24 million and is increasing by about 4 percent annually.

MONEY MATTERS

Kenyan currency is the shilling (Ksh), divided into 100 cents with nickel coins of 5 and 1 shilling and 50 cents, and copper coins of 10 and 5 cents. Notes are in denominations of 500, 200, 100, 50, 20 and 10 shillings. One Kenyan pound is 20 shillings. One 'bob' is one shilling.

Following the recent devaluations, exchange rates are fluctuating dramatically so check with different banks before changing your money. All currency transactions must be carried out at banks or licensed exchange facilities in hotels (where the rate is generally lower). If you decide to go for black market deals you risk not only losing your money but also arrest and imprisonment so be careful. It's safest to bring traveller's cheques rather than large amounts of cash.

You can take only 200 shillings out of the country. All remaining currency must be re-converted at the airport (easy in theory but more difficult in practice) or handed over at the port of exit.

Keep US$20 in cash to pay for the mandatory international departure tax. If you pay in any other currency it will work out more expensive. Shillings are not acceptable for this tax.

Credit Cards

Visa, American Express, Diners, Barclays and Mastercard are accepted in many outlets. Ask for the payment voucher to be filled out in front of you and make sure you retrieve your carbon copy, particularly in restaurants and at the duty-free shop at the airport – there have been many incidents of fraudulent transactions made with faked signatures.

Tipping

In restaurants, it is usual to round your bill up to the nearest 100 shillings, even where the service charge is included (it's the only way to be sure that your waiter will receive the money). In private houses it is usual for guests to club together to tip 100 shillings per person, per day. Please don't forget to tip gardeners and *askaris* (guards) as their contribution to making your stay enjoyable is just as important as the more visible cooks and house servants. Car park, petrol pump and supermarket porters, etc, can be tipped 20 shillings.

Departure Taxes

A departure tax of US$20 must be paid in foreign currency when leaving the country by air. On internal flights, the departure tax is 50 shillings.

Banking Hours

Banks are open Monday to Friday 9am–2pm or 3pm; and the first and last Saturday of each month 9–11am. Outside these hours money can be changed in hotels or at the 24-hour bank at Jomo Kenyatta Airport in Nairobi.

GETTING AROUND

Public Transport

Travelling by *matatu* (brightly-painted public minibuses) does not necessarily entail certain death but you may come close to it. Like larger buses and coaches, they frequently overturn, often in rivers, killing or maiming all passengers. On good days, they are driven much too quickly and are involved in several near-misses.

Only use public transport if you are fully insured and prepared to suffer the consequences.

Beware local transport!

Taxis

Always use a taxi at night unless you're familiar with the city centres and driving in developing countries where the roads are riddled with potentially lethal potholes and are very badly lit. Kenatco (Tel: 02-338611/221561 in Nairobi or 011 311456/20340 in Mombasa) is a reliable company, with set fares per kilometre. In Nairobi, the black London taxis are also OK. Otherwise, negotiate the fare before you jump in or you could find yourself grossly overcharged.

Car Hire

Hiring your own vehicle is undoubtedly the best way to see Kenya. If you're worried about driving on unknown roads, hire a chauffeur too – it costs an extra Kshs 300–400 per day and saves worrying about leaving your valuables unattended or parking in the city centres. He will also be able to tell you everything you want to know about Kenyan politics, wildlife, etc (don't be shy to ask).

For most game parks and off-road driving, hire a four-wheel-drive vehicle, especially in the rainy season. A Suzuki is perfectly adequate for two people although you may find it claustrophobic for more than this. Range Rovers, Landrovers, Pajeros, Nissan Patrols, etc, are also readily available.

For driving around town Daihatsu Charades or something similar are quite adequate. At the coast an open-topped beach buggy is good for short trips but a more solid vehicle is advisable for longer distances or if you plan to leave any luggage unattended.

Avis, Hertz and Budget all have outlets in Kenya but you'll find better value for money at the smaller car-hire companies (see below). Try to reserve your vehicle well in advance. If the companies

The right vehicle is important

listed below can't help you, browse through the tourist literature on your first day in Kenya to see what special week, weekend or unlimited mileage rates are on offer elsewhere. Always ask to see the vehicle before you pay or you could find yourself with an old banger that hasn't been serviced for years and will let you down miles from help.

And check what you should do in the event of a breakdown. Some companies expect you to repair the vehicle and get back to Nairobi under your own steam, where they will reimburse your costs (keep the receipts). Others may come out to rescue you.

Most companies stipulate that drivers must be over 23 years of age and in possession of a valid national or international drivers' licence. You can't hire a car without taking out third party insurance at the same time. You should also take out Collision Damage Waiver (CDW) so that if you damage your own or another vehicle you are not liable to pay costs. Rates for CDW vary so check with individual companies.

Car Hire Companies

Nairobi:
Concorde Car Hire, PO Box 25053, Nairobi. Tel: 02-448953/4, Fax: Nairobi 02 448135
Kesana, PO Box 7154, Nairobi. Tel: 02-749062, Fax: Nairobi 02-741636, Telex: 25739

Mombasa:
Concorde Car Hire, PO Box 83183, Mombasa. Tel: 011-223502/315854, Fax: 011-228162
Kenya Rent a Car, PO Box 84868, Mombasa. Tel: 011-23048/20465

Parking

Car thefts are on the increase, even in daylight in the city centre. Try to park near embassies or government buildings where you see vehicles with red (diplomatic) numberplates. You can be sure that these are being watched by paid *askaris* (guards) who, for an extra 20 shillings, will also watch your vehicle.

Wherever you park, street youths will offer to watch over your car while you are away. Tip them 20 shillings on your return.

Trains

The main railway line runs from Mombasa on the coast to Kisumu in the west. The train service is slow but surprisingly reliable and very cheap. Two overnight trains run each day between Mombasa and Nairobi, leaving both stations promptly at 5pm and 7pm and arriving at 7.30am and 8am respectively.

The old-fashioned sleepers and dining car were once reminiscent of the olde-worlde elegance of the original settlers. Sadly, today it's all a bit shabby but it's still a relaxing and enjoyable way to travel, at least in one direction.

Reserve your tickets well in advance from Nairobi or Mombasa station (Tel: Nairobi 02-21211; 011-312220).

Planes

Kenya Airways operates regular flights between Nairobi and Mombasa and Malindi on Kenya Airways (Tel: Nairobi 02-229921; Mombasa 011-433326 or Malindi 0122-20192). Air Kenya operates regular flights between Nairobi and the Masai Mara, Amboseli, Lamu and Samburu from Wilson Airport on Langata Road. For details, contact Let's Go Travel, Tel: 02-340331/213033; PO Box 60342, Nairobi; Fax: 02-336890; Telex: 25440 Brusafari.

For flights from Malindi to Lamu, contact Skyways Kenya Ltd (Tel: Malindi 0122-20951) or Prestige Air Services (Tel: Malindi 0122-20860/1).

You can charter your own single or

twin-engine plane to fly anywhere in Kenya from Wilson Airport. Contact Safari Air Services (Tel: Nairobi 02-501211/4) or Boskovic Air Charters Ltd (Tel: Nairobi 02-501210/501219; PO Box 45646, Nairobi; Fax: Nairobi 02-505964). It's not as expensive as you might think.

There are luggage restrictions of 10–15kg (22–33lbs) per person on light aircraft.

COMMUNICATIONS

Post

Kenyan post is cheap and relatively efficient. The main post office in Nairobi is opposite City Square on Haile Selassie Avenue – the bridge over the road leads directly into it. It's open Monday–Friday 8am–12 noon, 2–4.30pm; Saturday 8am–12 noon. There are also branches on Moi Avenue and Tom Mboya Street.

In Mombasa, the main post office is on Digo Road between Makadera Road and Gusii Street. Stamps are also available in many hotels.

Telephones, Faxes, Telexes, etc

In Nairobi, international telephone calls, faxes, telexes, telegrams, etc, can be sent and received from Extelcoms on Haile Selassie Avenue (on the other side of the road from the central post office, down towards the railway station). Extelcoms is open from 8am–midnight. Take care of your belongings if you go in this area at night. You can also use hotel facilities but they are always much more expensive.

In Mombasa, you can make international calls from the post office on Digo Road.

Local and long-distance calls can be made from public phone boxes, if you can find one that is working. Place the coins ready in the slot before dialling – they will fall through automatically when your caller answers.

Be warned: the phone service is unreliable, especially during the rainy season.

Card telephones are more reliable than pay phones but cards are not always available. Ask at the post office or your hotel reception.

Useful telephone numbers

Country code for Kenya	254
Code for Nairobi	02
Code for Mombasa	011
Operator	900
Directory enquiries	991
International operator	0196
Fire, police, ambulance	999

MEDIA

There are three English language daily newspapers: the *Nation* (the best), the *Standard* and the *Kenya Times* (very pro-Moi). Foreign newspapers and magazines such as *Time*, *Newsweek* and *The Economist* are also available, either from street-sellers or in the larger hotels and shopping malls. For an insight into Kenyan politics read *The Weekly Review*, *Nairobi Law Monthly* or *Society* magazine.

The Kenya Broadcasting Corporation runs a (very mediocre) English-speaking radio station and television channel. The 24-hour, satellite-news network CNN interchanges with KTN, the second domestic TV channel, although coverage is blacked out if the story is unflattering to Kenya.

HOURS & HOLIDAYS

Business Hours

Offices and shops are open Monday–Friday from 8am–5.30pm with an hour's break for lunch around 1pm. Saturday hours are 8am-12.30pm. Small *dukas* (general stores) stay open much later.

At the coast trade may start as early as 7am but will be interrupted for a long siesta between 12.30 and 4pm; it then resumes until dark.

National Holidays

January 1	New Year's Day
March/April	Good Friday, Easter Monday
May 1	Labour Day

Celebrations

June 1	Madaraka Day (anniversary of self-government)
October 10	Nyayo Day (anniversary of President Moi's first inauguration)
October 20	Kenyatta Day (anniversary of Jomo Kenyatta's arrest and declaration of State of Emergency)
December 12	Jamhuri (Independence) Day
December 25	Christmas Day
December 26	Boxing Day
variable	Idd ul Fitr (Muslim holiday)

Festivals

January	International bill-fishing competition, Malindi
February	Mombasa fishing festival
March	Kenya open golf championship
Easter	Kenya Safari Rally
September	Nairobi Agricultural Show
October	Maulidi (Prophet's birthday) on Lamu – date varies
November	Malindi fishing festival
December	Boxing day races at Limuru Country Club

ACCOMMODATION

In the list of hotels which follows, $=under US$60 for a double, $$=$60–$100, and $$$=over $100.

Nairobi

The best hotels are all outside the town centre but it's well worth travelling the extra distance to stay in them.

THE KENTMERE CLUB
Limuru Road
PO Box 39508, Nairobi
Tel: 0154-41053/42101
The best value of all. English-style country inn in beautiful gardens 30 minutes from town. Boasts one of the best restaurants in Kenya. Golf, swimming, tennis and squash at nearby Limuru Club. $

SAFARI PARK HOTEL
Thika Road
PO Box 45038, Nairobi
Tel: 02-802493; Fax: 02-802477; Telex: 22114 SAFARO KE

The most beautiful hotel in Kenya – and all in African style. Set in 25 hectares (64 acres) of landscaped gardens with peacocks and a 2,000 sq metres (21,528 sq ft) lake-style swimming-pool. Twenty minutes from town. $$$

WINDSOR GOLF AND COUNTRY CLUB
Ridgeways, off Kiambu Road
PO Box 74957, Nairobi
Tel: 02-219784/217491; Fax: 02-217498
New hotel, about 20 minutes from town. Offers golf, swimming, squash, jogging track, tennis, gym, beauty parlour, boutiques, gift shops, etc. Very elegant American country club surroundings. Excellent restaurant. $$$

NAIROBI SERENA HOTEL
Nyerere Road
PO Box 46302, Nairobi. Tel: 02-725111; Fax: 02-725184; Telex: 22377
Within walking distance of town centre. Excellent swimming-pool, gym, sauna, steam bath. $$$

THE NORFOLK HOTEL
Harry Thuku Road
PO Box 40064, Nairobi. Tel: 02-335422; Fax: 02-336742; Telex: 22559
Swimming, gift shops, hairdressers, travel desk. Central to town. Where the old settlers used to stay. $$$

Mombasa

DIANI REEF HOTEL
South Beach
PO Box 35, Akunda, Mombasa. Tel: 0127-2723; Fax: 0127-2196; Telex: 21078
Swimming, tennis, mini-golf, watersports, squash, hairdressers all on offer. Seven restaurants. $$

SERENA BEACH HOTEL
North Beach
PO Box 90352, Shanzu, Mombasa
Tel: 0127-485721; Fax: 0127-485453; Telex: 21220
Swimming, tennis, squash, gift shops, hairdressers, watersports. $$

Serena Beach Hotel

NYALI BEACH HOTEL
North Beach
PO Box 90581, Mombasa
Tel: 011-471567; Fax: 011-471987;
Telex: 21241 NYALI KE
Swimming, tennis, golf, squash, disco, hairdressers, gift shops, water-sports, six restaurants, car hire desk. *$$*

Watamu

HEMINGWAYS
PO Box 267, Watamu
Tel: 0122-32624; Fax: 0122-32256;
Telex: 21373 HEMWAYS KEN
Undoubtedly the best hotel on the coast. Excellent service and food – particularly the smoked sail fish and spicy prawns served (free) at cocktail hour. Uncrowded beach. Few souvenir touts. Deep sea fishing and water-sports centre. *$$*

NIGHTLIFE

Don't come to Kenya if you're a party animal. On safari you'll be in bed by 10pm so that you can get up at the crack of dawn. In Nairobi, a good night out means dinner and perhaps a few spins at the casino. There are several discos but only **The Carnivore** approaches the sophistication of Western establishments. The average age at **Bubbles** (in the casino complex) is under 18, while **Florida 2000**, on Moi Avenue, and **The New Florida**, on Koinange Street, are little more than pick-up joints. If you're tempted, remember that 95 per cent of prostitutes are believed to be HIV positive, and that includes the gigolos down at the coast.

For a quieter evening in Nairobi, traditionalists might like the outside terrace of the **Norfolk Hotel** where the old colonialists used to drink. Go on a Friday night to see the resident white population in action. **Zanzee-Bar** on Moi Avenue, on the other hand, is popular with young people and has live music.

There are several cinemas which occasionally show good films; check the local papers for what's on.

At the coast, most hotels provide entertainment – fire-eaters, jugglers, dancing Samburu and snake charmers – with middle-of-the-road discos on Fridays.

HEALTH & EMERGENCIES

The name and times of the duty chemist can be found in the newspapers. If you need hospital treatment go either to Nairobi Hospital (Tel: 02-722160, Argwings Kodhek Road, Nairobi) or Aga Khan Hospital (Tel: 02-312953, Fifth Parklands Avenue, Nairobi). In Mombasa, go to the Coast General Hospital (Tel: 011-24111). These hospitals are expensive and you must pay a hefty deposit in advance unless you take all your insurance documents with you.

Africa Air Rescue

Provides emergency treatment and air transfer from the bush to a medical centre. One month's cover costs US$20. Tel: 02-337306/337504/215758; PO Box 41766, Nairobi; Fax Nairobi 02 210504: Telex: 25719 AIRESCUE. AMREF also provides a flying doctor service: Tel: 02-502699, Fax: 02-506112.

Water

Avoid drinking all tap water – even for cleaning your teeth. Hotels and lodges provide boiled or bottled water for this purpose but even so you may prefer to buy bottled mineral water.

Crime/Security

Poverty and crime are on the increase. Be careful day and night. Wearing expensive jewellery and carrying a camera or

bulging wallet are easy ways to make yourself a victim. Carry valuables in an old bag and dress down when walking around town. Be careful of strangers who may approach you with 'hard luck' stories. It's best to just say *Pole sana* (pronounced Polay sar-na and meaning 'I'm very sorry') and walk on. If you do get mugged, hand over whatever is required – avoiding risk of injury.

At night you should take taxis to and from your destination. Keep your car doors locked at all times, even while driving. Valuables and bags should be locked out of sight. Never stop to help broken-down vehicles or to give lifts to strangers. Don't drive after dark and always make sure you are back in Nairobi before sundown.

On safari up country, try to travel with more than one vehicle, even if this means making a convoy with strangers.

SPORT

Beach Activities

Windsurfing, catamaraning, glass-bottom boating and sailing are possible at most hotels down at the coast.

Cycling

Cycles are for hire at most hotels at the coast. For cycling safaris, contact: Let's Go Travel (see *Planes*). For mountain bike safaris, contact Gametrackers (K) Ltd, Tel: 338927/222703/212830/1/2; PO Box 62042, Nairobi; Fax: 02-330903; Telex: 22258 TRACKER.

Canoeing

Contact Gametrackers (see *Cycling*).

Deep Sea Fishing

Beyond the reef enclosing the Kenya coast lie some of the best big game-fishing waters in the world. They teem with marlin, tuna, sailfish, wahoo, shark, barracuda, bonito and others. The fishing season lasts from July to May.

The best places to head out from are Watamu in the north or Shimoni to the south. In Watamu, Hemingways Deep Sea Fishing and Watersports Centre (Tel: 0122-32624; PO Box 267, Watamu; Fax: 0122-32256; Telex: 21373 HEMWAYS KE or Nairobi Bookings Ltd, Tel: 02-225255/219182; PO Box 56707, Nairobi; Fax: 02-216553; Telex: 25345 BOOKH KE). Boats can hold from 2–4 persons and can go for a full or half day. Food, beer and soft drinks, and the hire of all equipment, bait, life-jackets, etc, are included in the price. It's not cheap (approximately $560 per full day or about $416 per half day for big boats which hold four people) but it is well worth the experience.

If you like the idea of trying deep sea fishing but don't want to kill the fish, Hemingways also run a tag and release programme. So far over 300 marlin and sailfish have been tagged and released for scientific research purposes.

From Shimoni, the Pemba Channel Fishing Club (Tel: 011-313749 or Shimoni 2; PO Box 86952, Mombasa; Fax: 011-316875) have a 4m (46ft) Sportsfisherman Twin diesel 220 HP and three other boats for hire. These boats are also chartered by the Shimoni Reef Lodge (Tel: 011-471771; PO Box 82234, Mombasa; Fax: 011-471349; Telex: 21199 REEF KE).

Diving

There can be few better places to learn how to dive than Watamu, Shimoni or Malindi, and internationally recognised Professional Association of Diving Instructors (PADI) courses can be arranged at most hotels. You'll spend the first day getting used to the equipment and learning safety procedures in a swimming-

A great place to learn to dive

pool. After that you'll be out diving off the reef. It takes four days to complete the open water course. You can also take the advanced course (three days), rescue diver course (minimum seven days) or dive master course (minimum two weeks).

If you're an experienced diver, the underwater cliffs in the clear seas off Shimoni are renowned for the diversity of fishlife. There are also underwater caves in Mida Creek to the south of Watamu which are home to giant rock cod (tewa) weighing up to 400kg (880lbs) but beware the underwater currents.

Snorkelling

The best snorkelling is in the Kisite-Mpunguti Marine Reserve off Shimoni in the south (see Itinerary 19) where the water is crystal clear and the coral is still fairly undisturbed. The Watamu Marine Reserve in the north is a good second-best. However, conservationists are concerned that siltation from the Sabaki river north of Malindi is slowly suffocating the coral polyps and preventing it from feeding. For the time being, though, there are plenty of fish and marine flora.

Freshwater Fishing

At Naivasha, contact Naivasha Lake Hotel (Tel: 02-335807); in the Aberdares, contact Aberdare Country Club (Tel: 0171-55620 or 02-216940); in Nanyuki, contact Mount Kenya Safari Club (Tel: 02-216940); in Watamu, contact Hemingways Deep Sea Fishing and Watersports Centre (see *Deep Sea Fishing*).

Golf

There are five golf courses in and around Nairobi: Karen Golf Club (Tel: 02-882801/2); Muthaiga Golf Club (Tel: 02-762414); Royal Nairobi Golf Club (Tel: 02-725769); Limuru Country Club (Tel: 0154-40033) and Windsor Golf and Country Club (Tel: 02-219784/217497/217499).

Tennis

In Nairobi, there are two hard courts at Utalii Hotel on the Thika Road (Tel: Nairobi 02-802540). You can also play at Windsor Golf and Country Club (see *Golf*) and Limuru Country Club (see *Golf*).There are also plenty of courts in Mombasa. Check with your hotel.

Riding

Join a one-day or a half-day trek out from Karen to the edge of the Rift Valley (Tel: 02-225255). Horseback safaris on the outskirts of the Masai Mara can be organised through Tony Church (Tel: 02-891168/726209) and Voorspuys Horseback Safaris (PO Box 502739, Nairobi; Fax: 02-502739).

Walking

Walking safaris outside the Masai Mara can be organised through Chartered Expeditions Kenya Ltd (Tel: 02-333285 or 212370/1/2; PO Box 61542, Nairobi; Fax: 02-228875; Telex: 22992). Other walking safaris can be organised through Gametrackers (see *Cycling*) and Kentrak (info from Let's Go Travel – see *Planes*).

Waterskiing

You can waterski on Lakes Naivasha and Baringo and in Mida Creek behind Watamu. In Naivasha, contact Naivasha Lake Hotel (see *Freshwater fishing*); in Baringo, contact Saruni Island Camp (see Itinerary 10); in Watamu, contact Hemingways Deep Sea Fishing and Watersports Centre (see *Deep Sea Fishing*).

Whitewater Rafting

To raft down the Athi or Tana river, on safaris lasting from one day to two weeks or more, contact Savage Wilderness Safaris Ltd (Tel: 02-521590; PO Box 44827, Nairobi; Fax: 02-501754).

USEFUL INFORMATION

Photography

Slide and print film and processing facilities are widely available. Don't forget to bring a spare camera battery, a lens hood, ultra-violet filter and a telephoto lens (200–300mm). It can get very dusty on safari so a good camera bag is useful.

In Nairobi, Expo Camera Centre (Tel: 02-221797/336921) on Kaunda Street repairs cameras and hires out equipment.

Bookshops

The best bookshop in Nairobi is the Nation Bookshop (Tel: 02-333507/224619) on the corner of Kenyatta Avenue and Moi Avenue, just round from the New Stanley Hotel. The Text Book Centre (Tel: 02-747405) in the Sarit Centre, Westlands, is also very good.

Maps

Survey of Kenya maps are the best and are available from the Public Map Office on Harambee Avenue (Monday to Friday 8am–1pm and 2–5pm). The Macmillan Travellers' Map of Kenya (with street plans of Nairobi and Mombasa and a map of Nairobi National Park) is suitable for itineraries in this book. So are their maps of Masai Mara National Reserve, Amboseli, and Tsavo East and West National Parks. Tourist Maps (K) Ltd publish maps of Lake Nakuru National Park and a Nairobi map. (Maps available in bookshops and hotel gift shops.)

Tourist Offices

For information on tours and excursions in Kenya call into Let's Go Travel (see under *Planes*) or any other travel agency.

Consulates

Australia Development House, Moi Avenue, PO Box 30360, Nairobi. Tel: Nairobi 02-334666/334672.

Canada Comcraft House, Haile Selassie Avenue, PO Box 41748, Nairobi. Tel: Nairobi 02-334033/4/5/6.

France Embassy House, Harambee Avenue, PO Box 41784, Nairobi. Tel: Nairobi 02-339783/4 or 339973/4.

Germany Embassy House, Harambee Avenue, PO Box 30180, Nairobi. Tel: Nairobi 02-221316/227069.

Netherlands Uchumi House, Nkrumah Avenue, PO Box 41537, Nairobi. Tel: Nairobi 02-332420/227111/2.

Spain Bruce House, Standard Street, PO Box 45503, Nairobi. Tel: Nairobi 02-336330/335711.

United Kingdom Bruce House, Standard Street, PO Box 30465, Nairobi. Tel: Nairobi 02-335944/335960.

United States US Embassy Building, Moi Avenue, PO Box 30137, Nairobi. Tel: Nairobi 02-334141/2/3/4/5/6/7/8/9/50.

USEFUL KISWAHILI PHRASES

Hello	*Jambo*
How are you?	*Habari gani?*
Fine/very well/good	*Nzuri*
Bad	*Mbaya*
Thank you	*Asante sana*
Please	*Tafadhali*
Goodbye	*Kwaheri*
Welcome	*Karibu*
Sorry	*Pole*
Very	*Sana*
Who?	*Nani?*
What?	*Nini?*
Where?	*Wapi?*
When?	*Lini?*
Why?	*Kwa nini?*
How?	*Vipi?*
A lot	*Nyingi*
More	*Ngine*
Today	*Leo*
Tomorrow	*Kesho*

Now	Sasa
Yes	Ndiyo
No	Hapana

Food and drink

Food	Chakula
Drink	Kinwaje
Coffee	Kahawa
Tea	Chai
Milk	Maziwa
Water	Maji
Sugar	Sukari
Cold	Baridi
Beer/alcohol	Pombe
Small	Kidogo
Big	Kubwa
Meat	Nyama
Grilled meat	Nyama choma
Fruit	Matunda
Fish	Samaki
Salt	Chumvi

At the Market

How much?	Bei gani? or Pesa ngapi?
Expensive	Ghali
Money	Pesa
Shop	Duka
Market	Soko

Numbers

1	Moja	7	Saba
2	Mbili	8	Nane
3	Tatu	9	Tisa
4	Nne	10	Kumi
5	Tano	11	Kumi na moja
6	Sita	12	Kumi na mbili

13	Kumi na tatu, etc	40	Arobaini
20	Ishirini	50	Hamsini
21	Ishirini na moja	100	Mia moja
30	Thelathini	1,000	Elfu moja

Phrases

Good morning	Habari ya asabuhi? reply: Nzuri, asante
What is your name?	Jina lake ni nani?
My name is...	Jina langu ni...
Right	Kulia
Left	Kushoto
Straight ahead	Moja ku moja
Wait a minute	Ngoja kidogo
Where is the toilet?	Choo iko wapi?

FURTHER READING

Insight Guide: Kenya and *Insight Guide: East African Wildlife*, Safari Special. Published by Apa Publications.

Adamson, Joy; *Peoples of Kenya*, London 1967.

Blixen, Karen; *Out of Africa* (1938).

Blixen, Karen; *Letters form Africa 1914–1931*, (Frans Lasson ed), London 1982.

Dorst, Jean and Dandelot, Pierre; *A Field Guide to the Larger Mammals of Africa*, London 1970.

Haltenorth, Theodore and Diller, Helmut; *A Field Guide to the Mammals of Africa, including Madagascar*, London 1980.

Huxley, Elspeth (ed); *Nine Faces of Kenya*, London 1991.

Miller, Charles; *The Lunatic Express*, London 1971.

Au revoir

Index

V, W

ACKNOWLEDGMENTS

This book would not have been possible without the help of Rudi van Dijck, Marion Op het Veld, Scott Vaughn and Jorge Illueca of the United Nations Environment Programme, and my assistants, Alice Mutonye and Nell.

Photography	**David Keith Jones/Images of Africa**
	and
Page 68	**Karl Ammann**
21T, 23, 24B, 35T, 37T, 38T, 38B, 44, 48, 49T, 52T, 59T, 64, 65T, 67B, 78, 80, 86, 87	**Bodo Bondzio**
89	**Zdenka Bondzio**
18	**Marti Colley**
37B	**Carla Signorini Jones**
10/11, 13, 17, 21B, 28T, 30T, 45B, 46, 53 54, 56, 57, 59B, 61, 62, 63T, 65B, 75, 79, 83, 84	**Wendy Stone**
Handwriting	**V. Barl**
Cover Design	**Klaus Geisler**
Cartography	**Berndtson & Berndtson**

Notes

INSIGHT GUIDES

COLORSET NUMBERS

You'll find the colorset number on the spine of each Insight Guide.

INSIGHT *POCKET* GUIDES

• • • • • • • • • • • • • • • • • • • •
United States: **Houghton Mifflin Company, Boston MA 02108**
Tel: (800) 2253362 Fax: (800) 4589501

Canada: **Thomas Allen & Son, 390 Steelcase Road East**
Markham, Ontario L3R 1G2
Tel: (416) 4759126 Fax: (416) 4756747

Great Britain: **GeoCenter UK, Hampshire RG22 4BJ**
Tel: (256) 817987 Fax: (256) 817988

Worldwide: **Höfer Communications Singapore 2262**
Tel: (65) 8612755 Fax: (65) 8616438

❝ I was first drawn to the Insight Guides by the excellent "Nepal" volume. I can think of no book which so effectively captures the essence of a country. Out of these pages leaped the Nepal I know – the captivating charm of a people and their culture. I've since discovered and enjoyed the entire Insight Guide Series. Each volume deals with a country or city in the same sensitive depth, which is nowhere more evident than in the superb photography. ❞

Sir Edmund Hillary